FREE THINGS FOR TEACHERS

FREE THINGS FOR TEACHERS

Susan Osborn

A Perigee Book

Perigee Books
are published by
The Putnam Publishing Group
200 Madison Avenue
New York, NY 10016

Library of Congress Cataloging-in-Publication Data

Osborn, Susan.
    Free things for teachers.

    1. Teaching—Aids and devices—Catalogs.
2. Free material—Catalogs.   I. Title.
LB1043.Z907   1987   016.3713'07'8   87-2409
ISBN 0-399-51334-5

Printed in the United States of America
1   2   3   4   5   6   7   8   9   10

CONTENTS

I. Introduction

Free Things for Teachers is one of the most valuable teaching resources you will ever own. Use it to fill your classroom with materials that will fascinate and motivate your students, and make your job easier. No item listed costs more than $2.00, and most are absolutely free!

Enriching your classroom and curriculum need not be expensive. Publishers, manufacturers, government agencies, and others offer booklets, posters, maps, worksheets, records, learning kits, teaching guides—and much more—just for the asking! You can receive author biographies from Harper & Row, a study in shoemaking from The Brown Shoe Company, a natural-foods cookbook for children from Frompovich Publications, rhythm instruments from The Children's Book and Music Center, and hundreds of other useful and creative teaching aids.

Free Things for Teachers is geared for the elementary school teacher, but we're sure that every teacher will find it a worthwhile source of information and ideas.

The authors have made sure that *Free Things for Teachers* is clear, practical, and easy to use. You will find extensive listings, complete ordering information, full descriptions of all materials, and helpful tips on how to use them.

Now you have the book that lets you bring the world into your classroom at the lowest possible cost. Enjoy using it, and have fun making your classroom brighter and more exciting than ever.

II. Animals and Pets

Kids and Cats

How many cats do you know? Do you know one with tiger stripes? And one with spots? And one with seven toes? Every cat is a little bit different from every other cat, but each one wants a kind owner.

The Animal Welfare Institute's illustrated, easy-to-read booklet tells children how to be good cat owners and what to do if your cat climbs up a tree. Single copies free.

Send: a postcard

Ask for: "Kittens and Cats"

Write to: Animal Welfare Institute
P.O. Box 3650
Washington, DC 20007

Animal Activities for People

Loving animals and helping them go hand in hand. "Animals and You" is designed to help children help animals. This 14-page booklet lists activities and animal projects, such as making a present for your pet and keeping an animal scrapbook, that children can do alone or in groups. Many of the activities can be incorporated into traditional lessons.

Send: $1.00

Ask for: "Animals and You"

Write to: MSPCA Humane Education
Division
Circulation Dept.
350 S. Huntington Ave.
Boston, MA 02130

How Pets and People Are Alike

"I have an animal friend who is an awful lot like me. Others say, 'You two are so different, you're like night and day,' but she and I know better."

Geared for the elementary-school-age reader, the bimonthly newsletter published by the Animal Rescue League of Boston offers straightforward advice on how to keep a pet happy and safe. The package includes a 1-year subscription to the newsletter, a color poster, and a membership card.

Send: $3.00

Ask for: newsletter

Write to: Animal Rescue League of Boston
Tremont and Arlington Sts.
P.O. Box 265
Boston, MA 02117

The Animal Connection

Having a guinea pig or a hamster to take care of can be a fun and valuable way of teaching students about the responsibilities and rewards of owning pets. As children care for their animals and watch them grow, they too experience the magic of growth and change, learning to respect the animals around them. Caring for a classroom pet is just one of many ways to teach kids to respect the animal kingdom. The MSPCA publishes this innovative teacher's booklet of classroom activities and discussions designed to foster humane attitudes among kids.

Send: $1.00

Ask for: "The Animal Connection"

Write to: MSPCA Humane Education Division
Circulation Dept.
350 S. Huntington Ave.
Boston, MA 02130

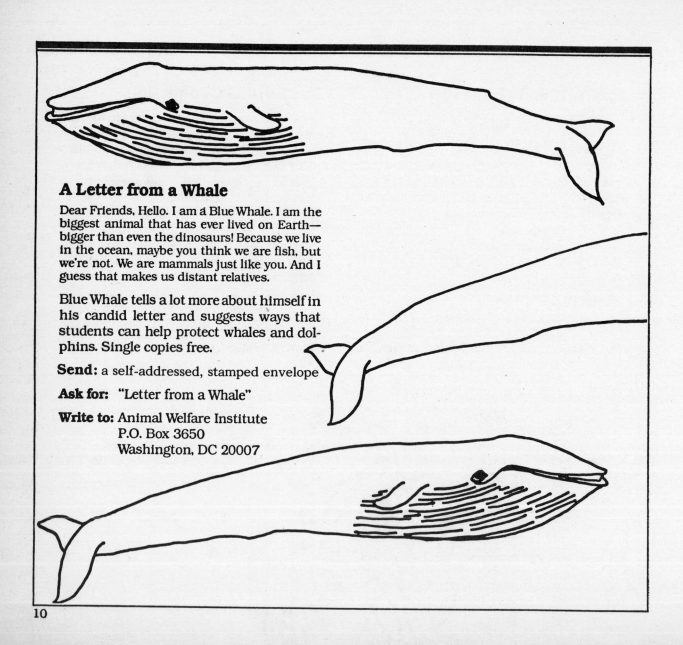

A Letter from a Whale

Dear Friends, Hello. I am a Blue Whale. I am the biggest animal that has ever lived on Earth— bigger than even the dinosaurs! Because we live in the ocean, maybe you think we are fish, but we're not. We are mammals just like you. And I guess that makes us distant relatives.

Blue Whale tells a lot more about himself in his candid letter and suggests ways that students can help protect whales and dolphins. Single copies free.

Send: a self-addressed, stamped envelope

Ask for: "Letter from a Whale"

Write to: Animal Welfare Institute
P.O. Box 3650
Washington, DC 20007

Kids and Their Canine Friends

If a child reads the Animal Welfare Institute's booklet on dogs and their masters, he or she will learn that dogs prefer good manners, need to eat and play, and require a shelter and regular doses of human kindness. Delightfully illustrated and easy to read. Single copies free.

Send: a postcard

Ask for: "You and Your Dog"

Write to: Animal Welfare Institute
P.O. Box 3650
Washington, DC 20007

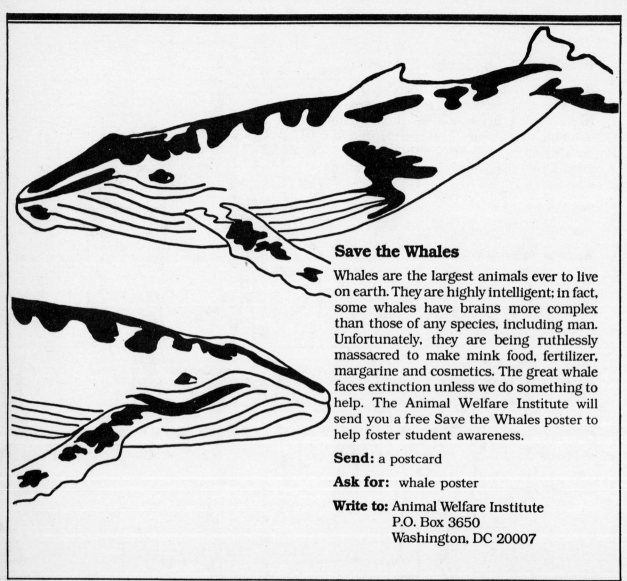

Save the Whales

Whales are the largest animals ever to live on earth. They are highly intelligent; in fact, some whales have brains more complex than those of any species, including man. Unfortunately, they are being ruthlessly massacred to make mink food, fertilizer, margarine and cosmetics. The great whale faces extinction unless we do something to help. The Animal Welfare Institute will send you a free Save the Whales poster to help foster student awareness.

Send: a postcard

Ask for: whale poster

Write to: Animal Welfare Institute
P.O. Box 3650
Washington, DC 20007

12

Living with Animals

The citizens of Critterton guide Carla and Michael Foster through their town as they examine the roles of animals and "animal people." The children learn much about the basic interdependency of animals and people and the cooperative nature of community living. A 23"-by-29" coloring poster ties the chapters together and illustrates the "complete" nature of the community. Suitable for intermediate readers.

Send: $1.50

Ask for: "Living with Animals" book and poster

Write to: MSPCA Humane Education Division
Circulation Dept.
350 S. Huntington Ave.
Boston, MA 02130

III. Arts and Crafts

Mythical Beasts Coloring Book

A noted designer and former editor of *American Artist* has created 30 attractive drawings of fabled creatures for this coloring book. Old favorites such as the mermaid, the centaur, and the phoenix are here, as well as the lesser-known basilisk, kraken, and manticore. Informative captions accompany each drawing.

Send: $2.50 (plus 85¢ postage & handling)

Ask for: "Mythical Beasts Coloring Book"

Write to: Dover Publications, Inc.
31 E. 2nd St.
Mineola, NY 11501

Fridolf Johnson

MYTHICAL BEASTS
COLORING BOOK

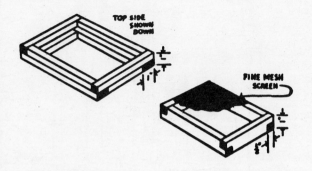

Making Paper by Hand

People have been making paper by hand for over 1,500 years, and now you and your students can too. Hammermill Papers will provide you with a packet that contains a booklet giving full illustrated instructions for the making of paper by hand. With the exception of the deckle and mold (a simple woodworking project), all the equipment necessary can be found in the home economics room.

Send: 25¢

Ask for: "How to Make Paper by Hand"

Write to: Hammermill Papers Group
Educational Services
P.O. Box 10050
Erie, PA 16533

Learning Art the Natural Way

Nature's own materials can often be the most instructive tools for introducing the basics in art. Geared for younger kids, this thoughtful book places emphasis on the utilization of mud, sand, and water for down-to-earth projects.

Send: $3.00

Ask for: "Mud, Sand, and Water"
(NAEYC No. 308)

Write to: The National Association for the Education of Young Children
1834 Connecticut Ave., N.W.
Washington, D.C. 20009

Chinese Papercuts

Papercuts from China are painstakingly handcut by skilled artisans with scissors or small knives. This art has been perfected through centuries of experimentation, and today's papercuts reflect both traditional and modern styles. China Books & Periodicals will send you a single papercut free. Use it to decorate your windows or cabinets.

Send: a postcard

Ask for: papercut

Write to: China Books & Periodicals, Inc.
2929 24th St.
San Francisco, CA 94110

Color Rackham's Fairy Tales

This coloring book presents 30 drawings and 17 Grimm fairy tales, including Hansel and Gretel, King Thrushbear, and Doctor Know-All. The full-page line illustrations will delight students and teachers alike.

Send: $2.95 (plus 85¢ postage & handling)

Ask for: "Rackham's Fairy Tale Coloring Book"

Write to: Dover Publications, Inc.
31 E. 2nd St.
Mineola, NY 11501

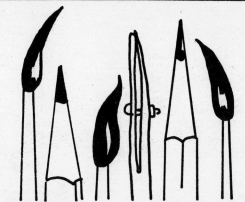

The Importance of Being Artistic in School

The Council for Basic Education, an organization whose primary purpose is the strengthening of teaching and learning in America, believes that the arts have a generative power, and in 1975, they added it to their canon of basic subjects. In this 32-page booklet, Dr. Jacques Barzun, professor emeritus at Columbia University, and Dr. Robert Saunders, art consultant in the Connecticut State Department of Education, attempt to explicate just how and where the arts fit into a basic curriculum.

Send: $2.00 (plus $2.00 postage & handling)

Ask for: "Art in Basic Education"

Write to: Council for Basic Education
725 15th St., N.W.
Washington, DC 20005

Art Task Cards

This set is ideal for helping students build skills and confidence in working with pastels and other art media. The 18 tasks outline methods and technique for drawing bottles, grapes, ships, and other fun-to-do projects which can be exhibited around the classroom after completion.

Send: $3.00 (plus $1.00 postage & handling)

Ask for: "Risk's Art Task Cards"

Write to: Teachers Exchange of San Francisco
28 Danview
San Francisco, CA 94131

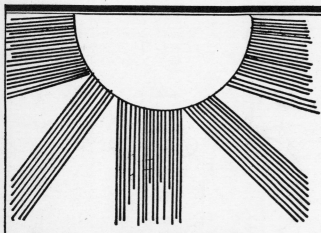

Sun-Powered Hot Dog Cooker

This experiment is meant to give you a glimpse of the future. It's a simple device that puts the sun's rays to work. With just a piece of lumber, a sheet of aluminum, a couple of nails, a pad of steel wool, a tube of household cement, a piece of aluminum foil, a ruler, a coat hanger, and a piece of sandpaper, you and your students can be the first ones in your town to have your very own solar-powered wienie roaster. Complete and detailed instructions are provided.

Send: 25¢ and a self-addressed, stamped envelope

Ask for: Solar Cooker Kit Directions

Write to: Energy Management Center
P.O. Box 190
Port Richey, FL 33568

Make Your Own Calendar

This imaginative coloring book is not only fun, but a sure-fire way to give your students a better understanding of numbers, days of the week, months, dates, seasons, and the concept of time. Because the calendar pages are blank, the book is a current calendar for any year.

Send: $2.25 (plus 85¢ postage & handling)

Ask for: "Make Your Own Calendar Coloring Book"

Write to: Dover Publications
31 E. 2nd St.
Mineola, NY 11501

Birthday Coloring Book

This 96-page book presents a drawing for each day—there are children playing, flowers, and outdoor scenes—each of which has been specially enlarged and rendered for coloring. A verse accompanies each, and there's space for kids to write in the birthdays of all their friends.

Send: $2.00 (plus 85¢ postage & handling)

Ask for: "Kate Greenaway's Birthday Coloring Book"

Write to: Dover Publications, Inc.
31 E. 2nd St.
Mineola, NY 11501

Color Benjamin Bunny

One morning a little rabbit sat on a bank. He pricked his ears and listened to the trit-trot, trit-trot of a pony. A gig was coming along the road; it was driven by Mr. McGregor, and beside him sat Mrs. McGregor in her best bonnet.

This charming coloring book includes the complete unabridged text from Beatrix Potter's original 1904 edition. The 29 black-and-white illustrations allow children to share in the fun of creating some of their favorite characters.

Send: $2.00 (plus 85¢ postage & handling)

Ask for: "The Tale of Benjamin Bunny Coloring Book"

Write to: Dover Publications, Inc.
31 E. 2nd St.
Mineola, NY 11501

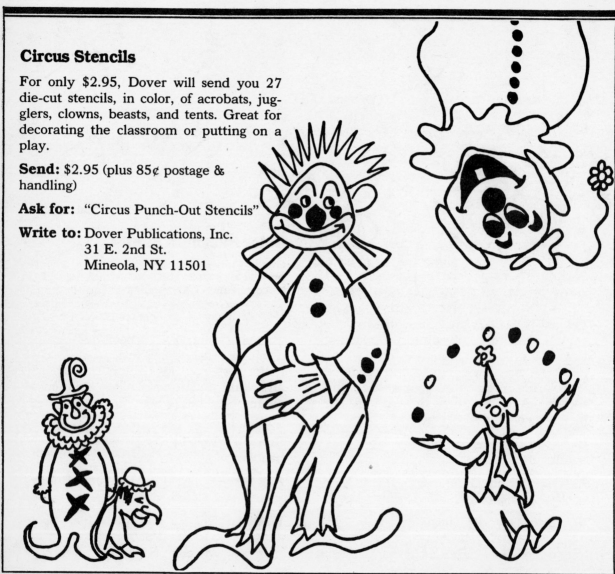

Circus Stencils

For only $2.95, Dover will send you 27 die-cut stencils, in color, of acrobats, jugglers, clowns, beasts, and tents. Great for decorating the classroom or putting on a play.

Send: $2.95 (plus 85¢ postage & handling)

Ask for: "Circus Punch-Out Stencils"

Write to: Dover Publications, Inc.
31 E. 2nd St.
Mineola, NY 11501

IV. Environment and Conservation

A Child's Garden

This two-color booklet lists a bounty of ideas for planting projects both in the classroom and out. Plants not only beautify the environment but also help develop a child's sense of ownership and pride. Turn your classroom into a green world and watch your students see, feel, and "grow" together. Limit one per teacher.

Send: a postcard

Ask for: "A Child's Garden"

Write to: Chevron Chemical Co.
Public Affairs
575 Market St.
San Francisco, CA 94119

Liven Up Your Classroom with a Pod of Whales

Tamar Griggs believes that science is not learned just by memory and experimentation, but also by touching the imagination and feelings of the child. She has developed a graphic way of learning about whales and conservation, and the aims of her workshop and suggested method of implementation are detailed in a flier offered by the Animal Welfare Institute. Single copies free.

Send: a self-addressed, stamped envelope

Ask for: "How to Liven Up Your Classroom with a Pod of Whales"

Write to: Animal Welfare Institute
P.O. Box 3650
Washington, DC 20007

Sierraecology Newsletter

In its ongoing efforts to bring issues of environmental concern to the public, the Sierra Club publishes a monthly newsletter designed specifically for grade school students. "Sierraecology" articles discuss current environmental threats and alternate energy sources and suggest inexpensive conservation-related activities for the classroom. School workshops and local cleanup efforts are advertised regularly, offering students an opportunity to actively join in the fight against environmental pollution.

Send: a postcard

Ask for: "Sierraecology"

Write to: Sierraecology
Sierra Club
Information Services
730 Polk St.
San Francisco, CA 94109

Learning About Renewable Energy

The earth's supply of natural resources such as coal and oil are well on their way to becoming exhausted. Now more than ever, it has become vitally important to find ecologically sound energy alternatives. Written especially for the younger audience, this educational pamphlet introduces children to alternate energy sources, such as wind, water, and solar power, emphasizing their importance to all of our futures.

Send: a postcard

Ask for: "Learning About Renewable Energy"

Write to: Renewable Energy Information
P.O. Box 8900
Silver Spring, MD 20907

Wildlife Needs You

Wild deer, sea otter, and other wild animals whose existence is being threatened by man-made pollution can do very little to protect themselves. But human beings can do quite a lot. This eye-opening fact sheet shows how various animals are being faced with possible extinction and describes the devastating long-term effects of pollution on the ecosystem. Complete with definitions and suggested activities, "Wildlife Needs You" will show children how they can help save the animals they love. Single copies free.

--tap the energy that lies in our coal reserves and maintain our way of life.

--protect the balance, beauty and usefulness of our environment.

Send: a postcard (75¢ for each additional copy)

Ask for: "Wildlife Needs You"

Write to: Sierra Club
Information Services
730 Polk St.
San Francisco, CA 94109

Color a Clean Environment

This coloring book is a fun and inexpensive tool for instilling environmental awareness in kids. Finished pictures can be displayed as a bright, personalized reminder of ways students can help keep their school, home, and neighborhood beautiful for everyone.

Send: 65¢.

Ask for: "Coloring Book"

Write to: Keep America Beautiful, Inc.
Communications Dept.
9 W. Broad St.
Stamford, CT 06902

Solar Reading List for Kids

The Conservation and Renewable Energy Inquiry and Referral Service has compiled a list of books about the sun and energy all of which are suitable for young readers, ages five through 12. The bibliography includes the title of the book, a summary, page length, and publisher. Help your students learn how the sun and earth can work together.

Send: a postcard

Ask for: "Solar Bibliography for Children"

Write to: Conservation and Renewable Energy Inquiry and Referral Service
P.O. Box 8900
Silver Spring, MD 20850

The Scrap Cycle

Fortunately, there's no limit to the number of times iron and steel can be recycled into new products. Old automobiles, farm equipment, ships, refrigerators, stoves, copper from car radiators, lead from batteries—almost any kind of obsolete metal can be prepared for a new use in a scrap metal plant.

In this delightfully illustrated pamphlet, children will learn about a scrap processing plant and about some of the ways that recycling scrap helps us and our environment.

Send: a postcard

Ask for: "The Scrap Book"

Write to: Institute of Scrap Iron and Steel, Inc.
1627 K St., N.W.
Washington, DC 20006

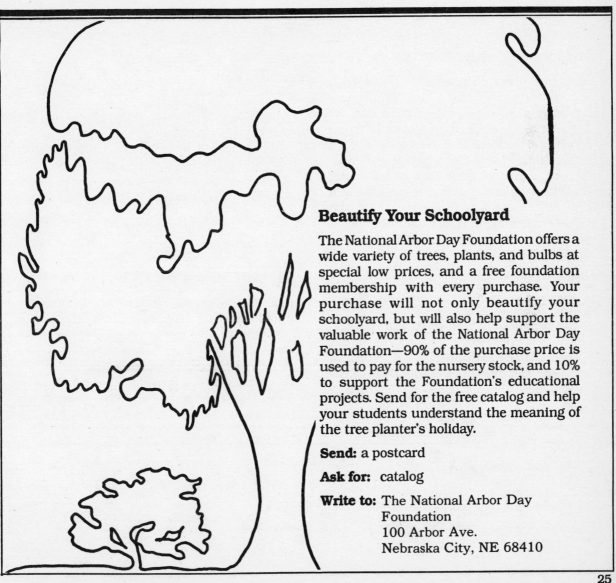

Beautify Your Schoolyard

The National Arbor Day Foundation offers a wide variety of trees, plants, and bulbs at special low prices, and a free foundation membership with every purchase. Your purchase will not only beautify your schoolyard, but will also help support the valuable work of the National Arbor Day Foundation—90% of the purchase price is used to pay for the nursery stock, and 10% to support the Foundation's educational projects. Send for the free catalog and help your students understand the meaning of the tree planter's holiday.

Send: a postcard

Ask for: catalog

Write to: The National Arbor Day
Foundation
100 Arbor Ave.
Nebraska City, NE 68410

25

Backyard Wildlife Kit

Invite wildlife into your schoolyard! With just a little money and a bit of planning a schoolyard or child's backyard can be transformed into a place attractive to all kinds of wildlife. The National Wildlife Federation, a nonprofit conservation education organization dedicated to informing Americans about the wise management of natural resources and the importance of a clean environment, offers an information packet that shows how to make your land an official backyard wildlife habitat.

Send: $1.00

Ask for: #79301

Write to: National Wildlife Federation
Dept. 916
1412 16th St., N.W.
Washington, DC 20036

Solar Energy and You

Children everywhere have felt the power of the sun warming their faces or tried to capture its rays in their hands. "Solar Energy and You" is an informative fact sheet which describes for students how solar panels are used to transform the sun's elusive rays into a valuable—and safe—source of energy.

Send: a postcard

Ask for: "Solar Energy and You"

Write to: Renewable Energy Information
P.O. Box 8900
Silver Spring, MD 20907

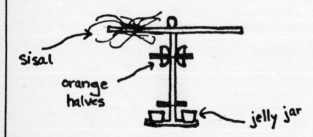

sisal

orange halves

jelly jar

Environmental Education Reading List

The Sierra Club's reading list provides a substantial amount of educational material on a wide variety of topical environmental issues. Teachers will find it very useful in supplementing their curricula.

Send: 20¢

Ask for: "Environmental Education Reading List for Young People"

Write to: Sierra Club
Information Services
730 Polk St.
San Francisco, CA 94209

Pollution Pointers for Kids

This two-page flier offers 25 projects teachers can perform with their students that will make everyone involved more aware of pollution and the ways we can help solve pollution problems. Suggestions include a litter art show, fancy can displays, and pollution contests. Up to 5 free copies free.

Send: a postard (5¢ each for over 5 copies)

Ask for: "Pollution Pointers for Elementary Students"

Write to: Keep America Beautiful, Inc.
Communications Dept.
9 W. Broad St.
Stamford, CT 06902

Environmental Hazards to Children

The child's developing body is much more vulnerable to pollution and poisonous substances than an adult's. Every day—whether playing with clay and paints, breathing heavily while running outside, or even just eating snacks with preservatives—kids are exposed to potentially harmful substances. This 28-page booklet describes both obvious and hidden environmental hazards to children and offers valuable advice on protecting children from them.

Send: $1.00

Ask for: pamphlet no. 600

Write to: Dept. FTT
Public Affairs Pamphlets
Public Affairs Committee, Inc.
381 Park Ave. South
New York, NY 10016

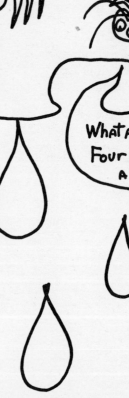

Arbor Day Is Back in Style

Each issue of "Arbor Day News" is devoted to a different tree-related theme. For example, one issue discussed Arbor Day celebrations, offering ideas used by schools and communities around the country. It also included a detailed plan for a school Arbor Day celebration, complete with tree-planting instructions. The newsletter is clearly written and extremely informative, and the foundation people will send you a single copy free.

Send: a postcard

Ask for: "Arbor Day News"

Write to: The National Arbor Day
Foundation
100 Arbor Ave.
Nebraska City, NE 68410

Birds and Recycling

Until recently, most bird books were written by people who worked in museums. They wrote about the dead birds in their collections and used long descriptions. But the birdwatching guide offered by the National Wildlife Federation is easy to read and has a simple way of picturing and identifying live birds. The 16-page booklet is 8″ by 10″ and includes a checklist of birds common to North America. Along with "Birdwatching," the federation will send you "Recycling," a booklet that explains the process of reusing wastes and suggests ways children can start a recycling project. Both are easy to read and educational.

Send: $1.00

Ask for: #79347

Write to: National Wildlife Federation
Dept. 916
1412 16th St., N.W.
Washington, DC 20036

V. Health and Safety

HE LIMPS AND WALKS FUNNY-

Helping Youth Decide

Sooner or later, growing children are faced with such physically and emotionally dangerous issues as smoking, drinking, and even pressure at school and at home. Written for parents and teachers, this book offers suggestions on how to discuss these sensitive subjects warmly and openly. Single copies in Spanish and English are available for free.

Send: a postcard

Ask for: "Helping Youth Decide"

Write to: The National Association of State Boards of Education P.O. Box 1176 Alexandria, VA 22313

Good Feet Mean Good Health

Little Johnny Sorefoot doesn't run or play with the other children. He limps and walks funny. When the teacher asks Johnny to join in the fun, he says, "My feet hurt." In this booklet published by the American Podiatric Medical Association, the Foot Doctor explains Johnny's problems and what can be done about them. A number of practical suggestions are offered. Johnny demonstrates them and shows that healthy feet really do make you feel better all over. Easy to read and amply illustrated.

Send: a postcard

Ask for: "Little Johnny Sorefoot"

Write to: American Podiatric Medical Association Dept. of Public Affairs 20 Chevy Chase Circle, N.W. Washington, DC 20015

A Montessori Approach to Alcoholism

If the children of alcoholics are to break the alcoholic life-style that is perpetuated from generation to generation, it is imperative that they develop their potential for creativity, initiative, independence, inner discipline, and self-confidence. The Montessori approach is ideal for treating the children of alcoholics. In a booklet published by the American Montessori Society, the authors explain why this approach is so effective and offer a careful analysis of elements of an educational environment that would best suit the child of an alcoholic. An intelligent study, important for teachers and parents alike.

Send: $1.00

Ask for: X109 "Social Work in Family Life Enrichment: The Children of Alcoholics—A Montessori Approach"

Write to: American Montessori Society
150 Fifth Ave.
New York, NY 10011

Help Your Students Make the Most of Their Eyes

Teachers are in a unique position to observe and detect vision difficulties. In the classroom, students must concentrate on a multitude of tasks requiring both near and distance visual skills. Effective and efficient vision is related to academic achievement, and observant teachers can help avoid problems. The American Optometric Association offers a free brochure outlining indications of possible visual impairment.

Send: request on school letterhead and a self-addressed, stamped business-size envelope

Ask for: "A Teacher's Guide to Vision Problems"

Write to: Communications Center
Dept. FTT
American Optometric Association
243 N. Lindbergh Blvd.
St. Louis, MO 63141

Bicycle Safety

This clearly written pamphlet describes in detail what young cyclists should know about maintaining and caring for their bikes. It also describes rules for safe cycling and illustrates proper turn signals. A bit of bike trivia is offered in the back (at the turn of the century, most police departments had bike patrolmen who arrested 12-mile-an-hour speedsters). An important guide for any cyclist.

Send: 50¢

Ask for: "Bicycle Safety Tips"

Write to: The National Easter Seal Society
2023 W. Ogden Ave.
Chicago, IL 60612

Kids and Drugs

Today, unlike a few years ago, every school-age child will sooner or later have to make a decision about whether or not to use drugs for recreational purposes. The Public Affairs Committee offers a straightforward primer for parents and teachers about children and drug abuse. This sympathetically written handbook recommends open communication between adults and children to discourage drug abuse and suggests that parents and teachers seek outside help if their efforts have failed. A list of commonly used drug terms is included.

Send: $1.00

Ask for: pamphlet no. 584

Write to: Dept. FTT
Public Affairs Pamphlets
Public Affairs Committee, Inc.
381 Park Ave. South
New York, NY 10016

Don't Touch!

As part of its nationwide campaign to inform the public about the dangers of explosives, the Institute of Makers of Explosives offers schools a free-loan program for its "Don't Touch!" videotape. The video is full of information on explosives and describes, among other things, what to do if you find a commercial blasting cap. Safety posters and a booklet of helpful information to supplement the video are provided as well. Should your school wish to purchase the video, special arrangements to reproduce "Don't Touch!" can be made at considerably reduced costs.

Send: request on school letterhead

Ask for: "Don't Touch!"

Write to: Institute of Makers of Explosives
1575 Eye St., N.W., Suite 550
Washington, DC 20005

Help for Students of Alcoholic Families

Alcoholics Anonymous, an organization dedicated to helping alcoholics achieve and maintain sobriety, also helps family and friends deal with the baffling and at times violent irrationality of the alcoholic. A student with an alcoholic relative can suffer from severe emotional problems that interfere with his or her ability to learn. In the pamphlet "Is There an Alcoholic in Your Life?" A.A. offers elementary and stimulating information as well as down-to-earth suggestions on how to deal with the alcoholic and where to go for further help.

Send: 15¢

Ask for: P-30

Write to: A.A. World Services, Inc.
P.O. Box 459
Grand Central Station
New York, NY 10163

Child Abuse and Neglect

The distressing problem of child abuse has far-reaching, harmful effects on both children and society. In this helpful pamphlet, the Public Affairs Committee examines the possible roots of child abuse and neglect. It also discusses legal developments and resources, and lists protective services and ways you can help prevent abuse and neglect. This is a valuable resource that will help enormously in identifying and getting effective help for abused children.

Send: $1.00

Ask for: pamphlet no. 588

Write to: Dept. FTT
Public Affairs Pamphlets
Public Affairs Committee, Inc.
381 Park Ave. South
New York, NY 10016

Why Kids Shouldn't Smoke

This 16-page brochure illustrates 12 reasons why kids shouldn't smoke. Besides the usual reasons, the author points out that smoking gives you tobacco breath and pollutes the air we breathe. The author suggests that the reader, when finished, pass the booklet on to an adult who smokes. An amusing and novel approach.

Send: 40¢

Ask for: "Why Kids Shouldn't Smoke"

Write to: C. J. Frompovich Publications
R.D. 1, Chestnut Rd.
Coopersburg, PA 18036

Sport Sense

With kids involved in so many varied and sophisticated sports, it is vital that they—as well as their parents and teachers—understand the increased nutritional needs of their athletically active bodies. Nancy Clark, nutritionist and author of "The Athlete's Kitchen," has written this common-sense approach pamphlet of nutritional tips for athletes. "Sport Sense" emphasizes the importance of exercise to good health, underlining the need to meet nutritional needs with carbohydrates and regular, well-balanced meals. Includes 5 well-balanced, tasty recipes.

Send: a postcard

Ask for: "Sport Sense"

Write to: Rice Council of America
Dept. "Sport Sense"
P.O. Box 740121
Houston, TX 77274

Posture Education

Reedco, "The Good Posture People," offers a reference sheet with suggestions and exercises for stimulating good posture in the classroom. By emphasizing good posture while standing, sitting, walking, lifting, and carrying, teachers may help prevent posture deformities and make the student a healthier person.

Send: a postcard

Ask for: "Basic Posture Patterns and Distortions with Adapted Exercise Programs"

Write to: Reedco, Inc.
P.O. Box 345
51 N. Fulton St.
Auburn, NY 13021

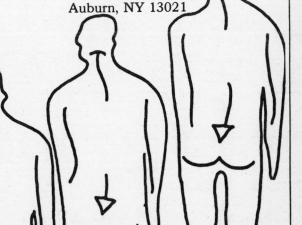

Watersafe

This 17-minute release on basic water safety techniques is available for loan on color film or videocassette free of charge. Olympic swimming champion Donna de Varona demonstrates for viewers safety tactics and methods of coping with emergencies while engaged in water events.

Send: a postcard

Ask for: a brochure

Write to: Modern Talking Picture
Service
5000 Park St. N.
St. Petersburg, FL 33709

Young People and A.A.

As every educator is aware, teenage and preteenage drinking is on the rise. A.A., the nationwide organization of alcoholics who share their experience in the hope that they may solve their common problem and help others recover, publishes an excellent pamphlet titled "Young People and A.A." In it, each of 10 members, ages 16 to 27, tells his or her own story and describes how the program works. If there's a problem drinker in your class, this booklet may help him or her to get back on the right track.

Send: 20¢

Ask for: P-4

Write to: A.A. World Services, Inc.
P.O. Box 459
Grand Central Station
New York, NY 10163

And, if you do need help or if you'd just like to talk to someone about your drinking, call us. We're in the phone book under Alcoholics Anonymous.

VI. Mathematics

Book of Tables and Other Measures

More and more often, juice or soda is bought in liter containers, and goods are weighed in grams and measured in centimeters. In fact, the metric system is used in America almost as often as the imperial system, and we must be prepared to convert from one to the other at a moment's notice. The "Book of Tables and Other Measures" is a great way to learn how. The clear tables portrayed in this book provide an important reference and numerous tips for understanding and memorizing these conversions.

Send: $2.50 (plus $2.00 postage & handling)

Ask for: "Book of Tables and Other Measures"

Write to: Ladybird Books, Inc.
Chestnut St.
Lewiston, ME 04240

What Is Basic in Mathematics?

What mathematics do all children need for their lives in a society that depends on technology? What do they need in order to go on and learn the math they will need for access to jobs in industry and business? These questions and many others are answered in a 45-page booklet written by Stephen Willoughby, director of mathematics education at New York University. Willoughby is dedicated to helping children learn the usefulness of math in solving the problems of their daily lives.

Send: $2.00 (plus $2.00 postage & handling)

Ask for: "Teaching Mathematics: What Is Basic?"

Write to: Council for Basic Education
725 15th St., N.W.
Washington, DC 20005

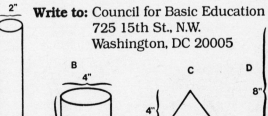

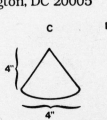

Fun with Numbers Coloring Book

What better way to teach counting and number skills? As children color these 45 charming illustrations, they will learn to count to twenty and perform simple addition and subtraction. Each scene teaches a basic lesson and is accompanied by a rhyme that helps children to remember the lesson.

Send: $2.50 (plus 85¢ postage & handling)

Ask for: "Fun with Numbers Coloring Book"

Write to: Dover Publications
31 E. 2nd St.
Mineola, NY 11501

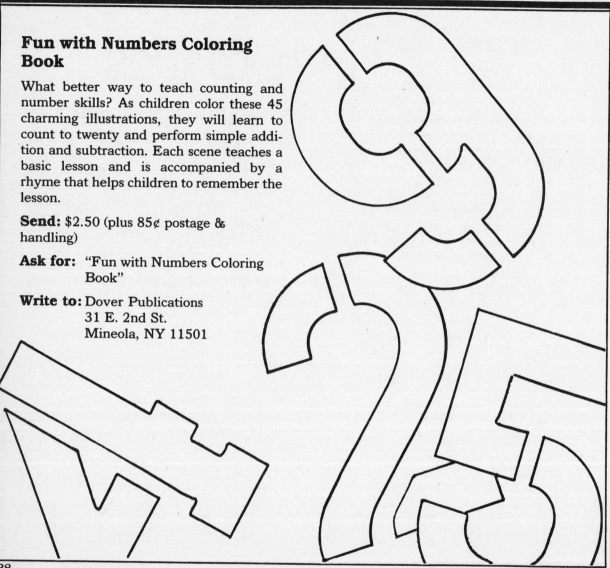

All About Computers

Computers come in all kinds of sizes and shapes, and are used to write, draw, measure, read prices, and do thousands of other things. This introductory book presents the basics of input, memory storage, decision-making, and data retrieval to 4th- through 6th-graders. Cleverly written and illustrated, it depicts the many wonderful ways computers enter our everyday lives and answers just about any question a child might have.

Send: $2.95

Ask for: "Computers: Sizes, Shapes and Flavors"

Write to: Banbury Books, Inc.
37 West Ave.
Wayne, PA 19087

Mastering 2 + 2

National test scores are down, particularly on items that deal with problem solving or with the ability to use math in real situations. The Cuisenaire Co. believes that the solution lies not in inventing new materials, but rather in making better use of the materials that have proven effective in the past. They claim that teachers who incorporate their manipulative material have a greater chance of producing math achievers than teachers who do not. Activities include chip trading, mathematical yarns, and relationshapes.

Send: a postcard

Ask for: catalog

Write to: Cuisenaire Co. of America, Inc.
12 Church St.
New Rochelle, NY 10805

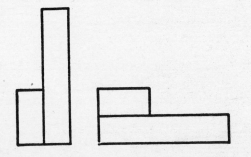

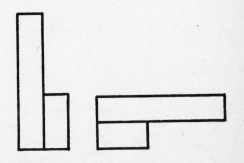

VII. Music

The Story of Music

Ladybird Books provides a series of 6 educational books about music for grade school children: "Musical Instruments," "Story of Music," "Great Composers" (2 volumes), "Ballet," and "The Story of the Theater." Each volume costs just $2.50 and provides easy-to-read information presented in an interesting, colorful format.

Send: $2.50 each (plus $2.00 postage & handling)

Ask for: title of desired book

Write to: Ladybird Books, Inc.
Chesnut St.
Lewiston, ME 04240

EasyReeding

Do you know how many presidents have played the harmonica? What was the first musical instrument played in outer space? What musical instrument did Benjamin Franklin invent? Hohner's new 16-page booklet on harmonicas—spiced throughout with numerous little-known fun facts—covers the history and production of harmonicas.

Send: a self-addressed, stamped legal-size envelope

Ask for: "EasyReeding"

Write to: Hohner, Inc.
Dept. FTT-1
P.O. Box 15035
Richmond, VA 23227

Music Instruction

Available for free, this catalog lists over 200 cassette, book, and video courses for guitar, bass, piano, drums, harmonica, banjo, mandolin, fiddle, and tinwhistle. You'll find instruction for all styles of music, as well as information on singing harmony parts.

Send: a postcard

Ask for: item no. 602

Write to: Parade
Dept. Z
P.O. Box 2529
Clinton, IA 52735

Music Austrian Style

From this colorful fold-out printed by the Austrian Press and Information Service, you and your students will learn about Minnesingers, Viennese opera composers, and contemporary Austrian musicians. Brief but informative biographies of Mozart, Haydn, the Strausses, Schönberg, Mahler, Bruckner, Berg, Hauer, Schubert, and Wolf are also included. The fold-out is attractively designed and shows photos of various musicially related items, including Beethoven's death mask, a program from *The Magic Flute,* and an ink drawing of the stage design for the 1975 Bregenz Festival. A fascinating way to introduce the world of Austrian music to students.

Send: a postcard

Ask for: "Austria Music"

Write to: Austrian Press and Information
Service
31 E. 69th St.
New York, NY 10021

Singing Rhymes

Kids of all ages love to sing rhymes such as "Georgie Porgie" and "Miss Mary Mack." "Singing Rhymes," published by Ladybird Books, includes several well-known playground rhymes as well as some lesser-known ones for children to learn. Melodies and lyrics are set in a wonderfully illustrated format both children and adults will love.

Send: $2.50 (plus $2.00 postage & handling)

Ask for: "Singing Rhymes"

Write to: Ladybird Books, Inc.
Chestnut St.
Lewiston, ME 04240

Piano Book of Cowboy Songs

Music educator Dolly Moon has set 21 well-known favorites, including "Home on the Range" and "On Top of Old Smoky," in simple arrangements designed specifically to introduce beginning students to the piano.

Send: $2.75 (plus 85¢ postage & handling)

Ask for: "My Very First Piano Book of Cowboy Songs"

Write to: Dover Publications, Inc.
31 E. 2nd St.
Mineola, NY 11501

VIII. Nutrition

Nutrition Workbook

With this attractively designed workbook, children can have fun coloring and solving word games while they learn about good eating habits. The 28-page book is filled with puzzles, riddles, word games, and enchanting illustrations. The book is NET approved and suitable for children aged six to 10.

Send: $1.50

Ask for: "Nutrition Workbook for Children"

Write to: C. J. Frompovich Publications
R.D. 1, Chestnut Rd.
Coopersburg, PA 18036

Bread Puzzle

This 10-piece puzzle in the shape of a slice of bread tells students what the various ingredients in bread can do for them. For example, niacin "makes me alert," riboflavin "helps me grow," and protein "helps build my body." A fun way to learn about nutrition.

Send: 50¢

Ask for: Bread Puzzle

Write to: American Institute of Baking
Communications Dept.
1213 Bakers Way
Manhattan, KS 66502

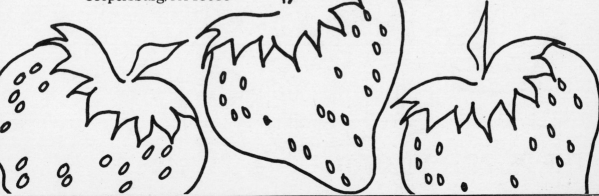

Kids Cooking Naturally

This delightfully illustrated cookbook will encourage the very young cook (ages seven to 10) to prepare nutritious and delicious meals. Recipes include yogurt sundaes, no-chocolate chocolate milk, chef's salad, and fruity tootie. Membership application for the Kids Cooking Naturally Club (no dues!) is included.

Send: $1.50

Ask for: "Kids Cooking Naturally"

Write to: C. J. Frompovich Publications
R.D. 1, Chestnut Rd.
Coopersburg, PA 18036

The Great Food Show

Through animated stories of knights and dragons, Red Riding Hood, and other favorites, kids are introduced to the four food groups and to the importance of balanced meals and eating a good breakfast. This 15-minute 16mm film is highlighted with bright music and dialogue and is available on free loan from the Modern Talking Picture Service library closest to your school.

Send: a postcard

Ask for: a catalog

Write to: Modern Talking Picture Service
5000 Park St. N.
St. Petersburg, FL 33709

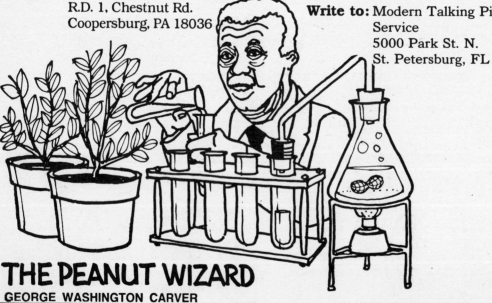

THE PEANUT WIZARD
GEORGE WASHINGTON CARVER

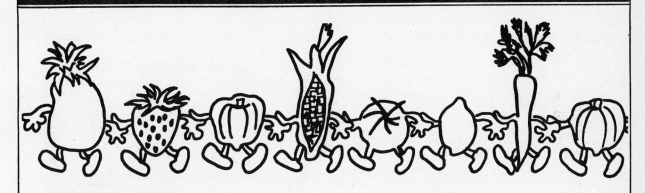

Creative Nutrition

One of the least enviable aspects of American society is our abnormally high per-capita consumption of refined sugar. In a booklet titled "The Junk Food Alternative," three parents suggest ways of cutting down on fats, cholesterol, and bologna in school lunches. This attractively illustrated booklet is filled with good ideas as well as recipes for nutritious pancakes, carob chip cookies, and natural fruit juice–sweetened gelatin.

Send: 50¢

Ask for: X061 "Creative Nutrition, The Junk Food Alternative"

Write to: American Montessori Society
150 Fifth Ave.
New York, NY 10011

Packing Brown Bags with Nutrition

Phony Bolognie
  Ham and Cheese
Isn't there anything different
  For my lunch bag—
Please!!!

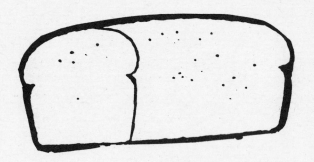

There's no reason children who have to "brown-bag it" should be deprived of nutritious foods, and in this imaginative, illustrated guide, the author suggests many delicious ways to make sandwiches more healthful and interesting. Order a pamphlet and send it home with your little brown-baggers.

Send: 30¢

Ask for: "Brown Bagging It"

Write to: C. J. Frompovich Publications
R.D. 1, Chestnut Rd.
Coopersburg, PA 18036

How Is Bread Made?

"Bread in the Making," a colorfully illustrated booklet published by the American Institute of Baking, takes readers on a tour of a bread factory. Mr. Blake, their guide, talks about ingredients, mixing, dividing and rounding, proofing, de-panning, cooling, slicing, wrapping, and delivering. Fun for children to read alone or in groups.

Send: 50¢

Ask for: "Bread in the Making"

Write to: American Institute of Baking
Communications Dept.
1213 Bakers Way
Manhattan, KS 66502

Rice Plus

Rice is one of the oldest sources of food in the world, having been cultivated since 2800 B.C.! "Facts About US Rice," published by the Rice Council, describes the history and production of rice in the United States, explaining how rice is still an important nutritional staple today. "Cooking Healthy with Rice" includes several delicious recipes for rice, while "Brown Rice" supplies additional recipes and information.

Send: a self-addressed, stamped business-size envelope

Ask for: booklet by name

Write to: Rice Council of America
Dept. (name of booklet)
P.O. Box 740121
Houston, TX 77274

A First Cookbook for Children

This fully illustrated beginner's cookbook requires little or no parental or teacher supervision. Easy-to-follow instructions for 60 tasty recipes are accompanied by clear explanations of ingredients and utensils.

Send: $2.75 (plus 85¢ postage & handling)

Ask for: "A First Cookbook for Children"

Write to: Dover Publications, Inc.
31 E. 2nd St.
Mineola, NY 11501

IX. Parents and Community

Community Cleanup

A cleanup campaign is a good way of improving the local environment, but to be effective, it takes planning. Keep America Beautiful's outline spells it out for you and tells you the government officials to contact, how to prepare a grid map of a community for cleanup-crew assignments, how to recruit volunteers, how to secure the cooperation of business and industry, how to publicize the campaign, how to co-ordinate volunteers, and the necessary follow-up tasks. Up to 5 copies free.

Send: a postcard (5¢ each for over 5 copies)

Write to: Keep America Beautiful, Inc.
Communications Dept.
9 W. Broad St.
Stamford, CT 06902

How to Tell Your Child About Sex

Sex-related issues inevitably arise at school and at home, regardless of whether or not sex education is taught in a given classroom. "How to Tell Your Child About Sex" provides a clear, practical approach to handling this sensitive subject for both parents and teachers. How and when to broach the subject with your child are discussed, and frequently asked questions are dealt with in a straightforward manner.

Send: $1.00

Ask for: no. 149

Write to: Dept. FTT
Public Affairs Pamphlets
Public Affairs Committee, Inc.
381 Park Ave. South
New York, NY 10016

Getting Help for a Disabled Child

This 28-page pamphlet by the Public Affairs Office provides a wealth of important information on everything from tips and techniques for diagnosing disabilities to support groups for parents, and legal rights of disabled children and their parents in the public educational system. An invaluable reference.

Send: $1.00

Ask for: pamphlet no. 615

Write to: Dept. FTT
Public Affairs Pamphlets
Public Affairs Committee, Inc.
381 Park Ave. South
New York, NY 10016

School Crime

During World War II and the 1950s, crime and delinquency rates remained relatively stable, but by the 1960s, the rate of crime increased to a point where it demanded public concern. The ERIC fact sheet on school crime and disruption discusses the extent of violence in the schools, the relationship between school crime and the community, and the action schools can take to create a safe and secure learning environment.

Send: a postcard

Ask for: Fact Sheet Number 1

Write to: ERIC Clearinghouse on
Urban Education
Box 40
Teachers College
Columbia University
New York, NY 10027

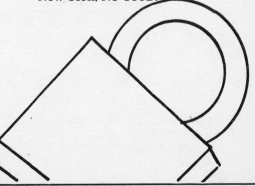

The Community School and Montessori

The community-school concept can be traced back to Plato and is based on the idea that learning is a lifelong process that does not end with a diploma. The Montessori approach promotes the idea that the child carries within him the potentialities of the person he will become. One of the basic premises of the Montessori method is that freedom to develop is achieved through the development of order and self-discipline. Both approaches aim for self attainment. In a booklet published by the American Montessori Society, the authors outline the fundamental principles of these two approaches and describe possible methods of implementation.

Send: $1.00

Ask for: X103 "A Montessori Program in a Community School System"

Write to: American Montessori Society
150 Fifth Ave.
New York, NY 10011

Taking the Pressure off Kids

Children learn not only through planned educational activities but also by experiencing and imitating the feelings and values of important adults around them. It is no surprise then that the stresses of parents and teachers are reflected in their children. In the Public Affairs Committee pamphlet "Pressures on Children," Alicerose Barman, a consultant in child development, describes ways of avoiding potentially destructive situations and refers readers to other pamphlets that describe specific problems in detail.

Send: $1.00

Ask for: pamphlet no. 589

Write to: Dept. FTT
Public Affairs Pamphlets
Public Affairs Committee, Inc.
381 Park Ave. South
New York, NY 10016

Growing Without Schooling

"Growing Without Schooling" is a bi-monthly magazine for people who have taken or wish to take their children out of school and have them learn at home. It includes articles by John Holt and other renowned educators, legal information, learning resources, advice from parents, and a copy of Holt's mail-order book list.

Send: $2.50

Ask for: sample of "Growing Without Schooling"

Write to: "Growing Without Schooling"
729 Boylston St.
Boston, MA 02116

X. Personal Development

Very Important Person's Workbook

I am a special person and there is nobody else like me anywhere. There are other girls and boys my size, my age, my color, my weight, but nobody else just like me. I can love people and things in just my very own way because I am alive here and now and that is what matters.

This very important children's book emphasizes in a clear and simple style the relationship between being alive and being important. A valuable aid to teaching about positive attitudes and self-worth. The book is replete with cartoon illustrations.

Send: $1.60

Ask for: "A Very Important Person's Workbook"

Write to: C. J. Frompovich Publications
R.D. 1, Chestnut Rd.
Coopersburg, PA 18036

Developing Humane Attitudes

An interest in and fondness for animal life is apparently a part of every child and it is during childhood and youth that the greatest good can be accomplished in instilling a knowledge of animals and an interest in our interdependence with animals.

The Animal Welfare Institute publishes a book that tells the instructor how to teach children about first aid and care of mice, gerbils, rabbits, birds, opposums, and other small animals. Single copies free.

Send: request on school letterhead

Ask for: "First Aid and Care of Small Animals"

Write to: Animal Welfare Institute
P.O. Box 3650
Washington, DC 20007

Supporting Children's Growth

Caring *can* make a difference. In this book by R.M. Warren, you'll find positive ways to help children deal with difficult issues such as divorce, abuse, and death.

Send: $3.00

Ask for: "Caring: Supporting Children's Growth" (NAEYC no. 213)

Write to: National Association for the Education of Young Children
1834 Connecticut Ave., N.W.
Washington, DC 20009

Braille for Seeing Children

Did you ever shut your eyes and run your fingers over a page of Braille printing? All the little raised dots seem to run together. Even if you knew the Braille alphabet, your fingers could not pick out each separate dot. But boys and girls who cannot see read stories in Braille. Their fingers are trained to be their eyes.

A special Braille edition of "My Weekly Reader" has been prepared by the American Printing House for the Blind so that seeing children may better understand how their blind friends see and write. Up to 5 copies free.

Send: a postcard (35¢ each for over 5 copies)

Ask for: "My Weekly Reader"

Write to: American Printing House for the Blind
1839 Frankfort Ave.
Louisville, KY 40206

Teaching Children to Care

Suppose an enormous lion suddenly appeared right in front of you, what would you do? Well, there probably wouldn't be much you could do except sit tight and hope that he was a good kind lion. And that's pretty well what all smaller creatures have to do when you suddenly appear in front of them—they all just hope that you are a good kind lion too.

In this delightfully illustrated pamphlet, the Animal Welfare Institute requests that children be good kind lions to birds, polliwogs, mice, rabbits, butterflies, and other small creatures. Single copies free.

Send: a self-addressed, stamped envelope

Ask for: "Good Kind Lion"

Write to: Animal Welfare Institute
P.O. Box 3650
Washington, DC 20007

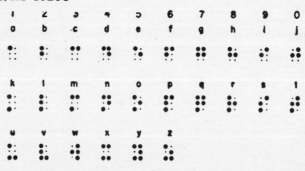

Great Great Grandmother

Great Grand Father

Great Grandmother

Grand Father

Grandmother

Grandmother

Father

Mother

child

child

Family Tree Workbook

Central to a child's world are the self and the family. Because of this innocent egocentricity, nothing could be more fascinating than tracing the how, why, where, and who of themselves. "My Family Tree Workbook" is an easy-to-use introduction to genealogy designed especially for children. Data pages for recording name, birthdate, place of birth, occupation, and other facts, as well as space for a photograph, are provided for great-grandparents, grandparents, parents, siblings, and the child. In addition, the author offers suggestions on collecting data, obtaining civil and church records, and tracing immigrant ancestors.

Send: $2.50 (plus 85¢ postage & handling)

Ask for: "My Family Tree Workbook"

Write to: Dover Publications, Inc.
31 E. 2nd St.
Mineola, NY 11501

XI. Publication Catalogs, Films, and Other A-V Aids

Toward a Bias-Free Society

The Council on Interracial Books for Children is dedicated to countering racism, sexism, and other forms of bias that children are habitually exposed to. Their catalog is free of charge and lists numerous filmstrips, books, pamphlets, lesson plans, and other curricula concerning issues of equality in school and society.

Send: a postcard

Ask for: catalog of publications

Write to: Council on Interracial Books
CIBC Resource Center
1841 Broadway
New York, NY 10023

Library of Congress

The Library of Congress is a resource every teacher should know about. Its stacks hold over 18 million books and pamphlets as well as newspapers, magazines, photographs, manuscripts, maps, posters, prints, films, television tapes, records, and lots more. The catalog lists books, pamphlets, serials, music, and literary recordings.

Send: a postcard

Ask for: "Publications in Print"

Write to: Library of Congress
Central Services Division, Box C
Washington, DC 20540

Reusable Text-Workbooks

Ann Arbor Publishers, the people who make reusable, nonconsumable text-workbooks, offer a wealth of materials for the teacher, including resource kits, arithmetic handbooks, ABC mazes, art activities, and many social and psychological aids, including a book on self-understanding and one on the need to fail. A valuable list.

Send: a postcard

Ask for: "Publications"

Write to: Ann Arbor Publishers, Inc.
P.O. Box 7249
Naples, FL 33941

Catalog of A-V Materials

Troll Associates, well known for their educational publications and children's book clubs, also provides films, slides, tapes, and countless other A-V materials on a wide variety of subjects. Teachers can get a copy of Troll's A-V catalog for free if it is delivered directly to their school.

Send: a postcard

Ask for: Catalog of A-V Materials

Write to: Troll Associates
320 Route 17
Mahwah, NJ 07430

Clearinghouse on Urban Education

ERIC stands for the Educational Resources Information Center. It is designed to provide users with ready access to primarily English-language literature dealing with education. ERIC's publications on urban education deal with topics such as decentralization, ethnicity, motivation, dropouts, human relations, learning patterns in the disadvantaged, and trends in bilingual education. The catalog includes an extensive list of annotated bibliographies and commissioned papers. Well worthwhile for any teacher trying to keep up to date.

Send: a postcard

Ask for: list of publications

Write to: ERIC Clearinghouse on Urban
Education
Box 40
Teachers College
Columbia University
New York, NY 10027

Great Kids' Books

Workman Publishing offers a wealth of exciting books for kids, including "Snips & Snails & Walnut Whales," "Steven Caney's Toy Book," and "The Boy and the Dove," the enchanting tale of a boy and his pet who must part, but who nevertheless find a new way of being together. Check out their catalog for books on crafts, hobbies, sports, and cooking.

Send: a postcard

Ask for: catalog

Write to: Workman Publishing Co., Inc.
1 W. 39th St.
New York, NY 10018

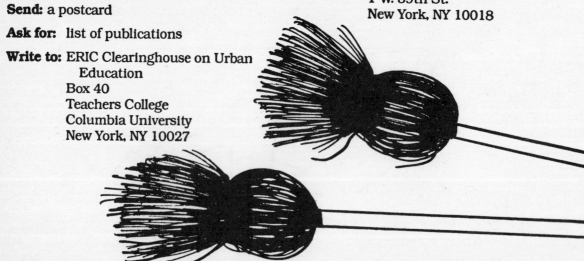

Public Affairs

The Public Affairs Committee was founded in 1935 "to develop new techniques to educate the American public on vital economic and social problems and to issue concise and interesting pamphlets dealing with such problems." On the basis of its informative booklets, the committee has, during the past four and one-half decades, gained a reputation for timeliness, accuracy, and readability. A catalog of inexpensive booklets, written for the general public on such subjects as alcohol and drug abuse, child development, family life, and mental health, is available free.

Send: a postcard

Ask for: public affairs pamphlets catalog

Write to: Dept. FTT
Public Affairs Pamphlets
Public Affairs Committee, Inc.
381 Park Ave. South
New York, NY 10016

Give Them the Big Picture

Giant Photos offers full-color posters and prints in an array of interesting subjects, most of which are available for $2.00. Teachers can bring their classrooms to life with scenes from China, Ireland, or Greece; the faces of Geronimo, Clara Barton, or Karl Marx; or illustrated versions of Patrick Henry's speech or the Preamble to the Declaration of Independence. A wide variety of sports and animal posters is also available.

Send: a postcard

Ask for: catalog

Write to: Giant Photos, Inc.
2402 N. Court St.
Rockford, IL 61103

Free-Loan Educational Films

One of the country's largest distributors of free-loan films and videocassettes offers a catalog of their merchandise available for many categories, e.g., energy and ecology, health and hygiene, home economics, safety and auto, science and technology, and more. Users pay return postage only.

Send: a postcard

Ask for: catalog of free-loan educational films

Write to: Modern Talking Picture Service
5000 Park St., N.
St. Petersburg, FL 33709

Info on Science, Math, and Environmental Ed.

The ERIC Clearinghouse for Science, Mathematics, and Environmental Education has processed several thousand documents and journal articles related to science, math, and environmental education. The materials include curriculum guides, research reports, evaluation reports, teacher's guides, and descriptions of educational and research programs. The annual bulletin and publications lists detail their activities and the information bulletins available.

Send: a postcard

Ask for: annual bulletin and publications lists

Write to: ERIC/SMEAC
Ohio State University
1200 Chambers Rd., Rm. 310
Columbus, OH 43212

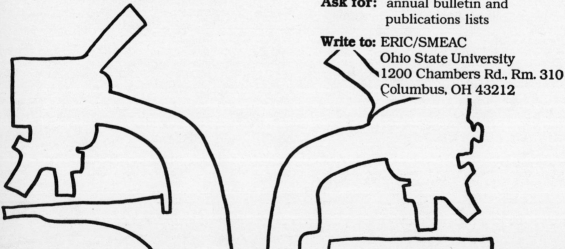

Unusual Teaching Aids

The Children's Book and Music Center is a unique source of phonograph records, books, multimedia, rhythm instruments, and enrichment materials suitable for children and teachers. The materials offered were chosen by trained professionals and represent the best available for all areas of curriculum.

Send: $1.00

Ask for: catalog

Write to: Children's Book and Music
Center
2500 Santa Monica Blvd.
Santa Monica, CA 90404

University Prints

The University Prints Co. offers hundreds of study sets in a wide range of subjects, most of which are priced at 30 illustrations for $1.50. Set titles include "Visits to Many Lands," "Visits to Famous Cities," "Visits to Great Museums," "Visits to Notable Eras," "Saints and Apostles," "Famous Churches and Cathedrals," "Fine Arts and Architecture," "History and Social Studies," "Epic Poetry," "Costumes of Many Lands," "Greek and Roman Theatres," and many more. All prints are 5½" by 8". This brochure will tell you the history of the company and lists the subject areas that are available.

Send: a postcard

Ask for: "Brochure: Special Topic Study Sets"

Write to: The University Prints Co.
21 East St.
P.O. Box 485
Winchester, MA 01890

Barron's

Although primarily known for their test preparation manuals and workbooks, Barron's also has a significant list of juvenile educational books, many of which cost under $5.00. Of special note are books done in collaboration with the renowned Bank Street College and Barron's wonderfully illustrated books on the four elements and the five senses.

Send: a postcard

Ask for: catalog of publications

Write to: Barron's
113 Crossways Park Dr.
Woodbury, NY 11797

Unusual Films and Publications

The Education Development Center, Inc., is a publicly supported nonprofit corporation engaged in educational research and development. Its catalog of films and publications lists a number of unusual materials, including films on Brazelton's studies of the newborn, films on Eskimos, films about life on a kibbutz, and publications on the informal classroom, curriculum improvement, and building a playground. Films can be rented or purchased, and many of the publications sell for under $2.00

Send: a postcard

Ask for: catalog of films and publications

Write to: EDC
39 Chapel St.
Newton, MA 02160

XII. Reading, Writing, and Language

News for You

New Readers Press offers "News for You," a weekly newspaper written in easy English for adults and children. Designed like a newspaper, it includes national and international news, legal and consumer tips, profiles of prominent people, sports coverage, and a 4-page worksheet to test your knowledge. Also, throughout the school year, a monthly supplement gives in-depth coverage of current topics. The paper is perfect for stimulating reluctant readers.

Send: a postcard

Ask for: "News for You" sample and "Instructor's Aid"

Write to: New Readers Press
1320 Jamesville Ave., Box 131
Syracuse, NY 13210

Write Your Own Story Coloring Book

This book presents 23 full-page illustrations for children to color, plus room for them to write in their own stories about the adventures of Penny, Mark, and Koko the clown. Each page can be a separate story, or they can be connected to make one long story.

Send: $2.50 (plus 85¢ postage & handling)

Ask for: "Write Your Own Story Coloring Book"

Write to: Dover Publications, Inc.
31 E. 2nd St.
Mineola, NY 11501

Phonics in Beginning Reading

It's a fact: Some approaches to teaching reading are better than others, and it's also well known that children learn to read more readily when they are taught by sound and rational methods. In its booklet on phonics and beginning reading, the Council for Basic Education describes the history of past follies in reading theory and practice, but its primary purpose is to inform teachers of the superiority of phonics- or code-based approaches over the whole-word method. A well-researched and valuable discussion.

Send: $1.00 (plus $2.50 postage & handling)

Ask for: "Phonics in Beginning Reading"

Write to: Council for Basic Education
725 15th St., N.W.
Washington, DC 20005

Short **a** says **ă** in apple

Short **e** says **ĕ** in elephant

Short **I** says **Ĭ** in Indian

Talking in Sioux

In this 111-page book, which includes 290 pictographs of the Sioux and Ojibway tribes, 525 signs of communication developed by the Blackfoot, Sioux, Cheyenne, and Arapahoe tribes are presented. Written instructions and diagrams are included, as well as information on how to make words and construct sentences.

Send: $2.95 (plus 85¢ postage & handling)

Ask for: "Indian Sign Language"

Write to: Dover Publications, Inc.
31 E. 2nd St.
Mineola, NY 11501

Word-Detecto Cards

This hidden-word puzzle game includes 16 cards, each with different groups of letters printed on it. From each group, the student must find as many words of three or more letters as he or she can. Suitable for grades three to six.

Send: $1.50 (plus $1.00 postage & handling)

Ask for: Word-Detecto Cards

Write to: Teachers Exchange of San Francisco
28 Dawnview
San Francisco, CA 94131

Hidden Messages

This fascinating publication teaches children in the 5th grade and up how to spot sexism, racism, materialism, and elitism in even the simplest stories. Package includes a fun lesson on "The Princess and the Pea," a student handout, a complete lesson plan, and explanatory pamphlets.

Send: $3.00

Ask for: "Hidden Messages in Children's Stories"

Write to: Council on Interracial Books CIBC Resource Center 1841 Broadway New York, NY 10023

Teaching Inner-City Kids to Read

By studying four schools that have successfully taught city kids to read, George Weber, associate director for the Council for Basic Education, has concluded that the failure that characterizes beginning readers in inner-city schools is the fault of the schools, not the children. The factors that account for the success of the four schools are strong leadership, high expectations, good atmosphere, strong emphasis on reading, additional reading personnel, use of phonics, individualization, and careful evaluation of pupil progress. Weber elaborates on his findings in this welcome 37-page booklet.

Send: $1.00 (plus $2.50 postage & handling)

Ask for: "Inner-City Children Can Be Taught to Read"

Write to: Council for Basic Education 725 15th St., N.W. Washington, DC 20005

NewsScan

"NewsScan" is the special newspaper for 5th- to 8th-graders that provides up-to-date coverage on current events, science, sports, and leisure. Features on young people in the news have particular appeal for students. Complete with a 4-page worksheet of puzzles, maps, vocabulary and writing exercises, and discussion questions, "NewsScan" is a great tool for teaching reading, social studies, and special ed.

Send: a postcard

Ask for: "NewsScan" free sample

Write to: New Readers Press
NewsScan Order Dept. 12
P.O. Box 131
Syracuse, NY 13210

Title Twister

The Title Twister card is a creative writing teacher's dream. The inner circle lists personalities: "me, myself, and I," "the mad scientist," "Uncle Grouch," and many more. The outer circle lists situations: "a wild, wild adventure with...," "one day in the life of...," "a narrow escape...," and many others. Kids can mix and match over 400 combinations. Sure to set young imaginations on fire.

Send: $1.00 (plus $1.00 postage & handling)

Ask for: Title Twister

Write to: Teachers Exchange of San
Francisco
600 35th Ave. (at Anza)
San Francisco, CA 94121

Why Teach Grammar?

Every native dialect reflects and perpetuates a local culture, and every student has the right to cherish that language and culture. But because a dialect represents just that, a local or limited culture, its value is bounded by its cultural milieu. If children are to understand, profit by, and contribute to the total culture of America, they must master the basic units of the language that we share. A child has a right to his own language, but he also has the right to know about the larger world in which he lives. These ideas and others are explicated in this formidable 42-page paper written by Kenneth Oliver, professor of English and comparative literature.

Send: $1.00 (plus $2.50 postage & handling)

Ask for: "A Sound Curriculum in English Grammar: Guidelines for Teachers and Parents"

Write to: Council for Basic Education
725 15th St., N.W.
Washington, DC 20005

Crossword Fun for Learning

The Teachers Exchange of San Francisco, specialists in innovative learning projects, now offers this package of 15 illustrated crossword puzzles for the intermediate grades. A protective coating for use with felt pens or crayons makes these puzzles reusable. Set A is for 4th- to 6th-graders, while set B is for use with 3rd- to 4th-graders. Helpful worksheets are also provided.

Send: $1.75 (plus $1.00 postage & handling)

Ask for: "Crossword Tasks" (specify set A or B)

Write to: Teachers Exchange of San Francisco
28 Dawnview
San Francisco, CA 94131

Get to Know Katherine Paterson

The wonderful thing about being a writer is that it gives you readers, readers who bring their own stories to the story you have written, people who have the power to take your mythic, unbelievable, ten-foot-high characters and fit them to the shape of their own lives.

So said Katherine Paterson during her National Book Award acceptance speech. In Harper & Row's four-page profile of this children's-book author, you will get to know a lot more about Paterson, as well as the titles of her books for young readers.

Send: a postcard

Ask for: Katherine Paterson bio

Write to: Crowell Junior Books
Dept. 128
10 E. 53rd St.
New York, NY 10022

XIII. Science

Jungle World!

For grades 4–12, this 48-page book is designed to accompany the Jungle World exhibit at the Bronx Zoo. Fully illustrated, with a glossary and bibliography for students and teachers, "Tropical Asian Animals" brings the wonderful Jungle World experience to the classroom.

Send: $1.25

Ask for: "Tropical Asian Animals"

Write to: Education Department
New York Zoological Society
Bronx Zoo
Bronx, NY 10460

Ornitholestes the Bird Robber

Ornitholestes (also called Coelurus) was one of the largest coelosaurs, somewhat larger than a man, but not nearly as heavy. He was capable of great speed and had sharp, hooked claws. Ornitholestes ("bird robber") lived during the Jurassic Period, and is thought to have fed upon small reptiles and early birds.

This carefully researched coloring book includes over 40 drawings of dinosaurs, archosaurs, fossil birds, and sea turtles. Each illustration is accompanied by an informative caption.

Send: $2.50 (plus 85¢ postage & handling)

Ask for: "The Dinosaur Coloring Book"

Write to: Dover Publications, Inc.
31 E. 2nd St.
Mineola, NY 11501

How to Forecast the Weather

Just watch the clouds, note the wind direction, and read the information on this chart, and you will be able to forecast the weather. The study of morning and evening skies can become an interesting hobby, and by comparing what you see in this chart, you and your students can become amateur weather prophets.

Send: $2.00

Ask for: Chart B (6th grade and up)
Chart C (grades 3–5)

Write to: Cloud Chart, Inc.
P.O. Box 29294
Richmond, VA 23233

Space Photos

Space Photos of Houston, Texas, will send you slides of outer space as seen through the eyes of the cameras on the various Apollo, Voyager, Viking, and Mariner missions. These slides, photos, posters, postcards, and prints document one of the most thrilling eras in recent history: man's conquest of space. Space Photos also supplies commemorative coins, covers, and emblems. Simply perusing the catalog is an educational experience.

Send: $2.00

Ask for: catalog

Write to: Space Photos
2608 Sunset Blvd.
Houston, TX 77005

All About Fish

You'd be surprised at the number and variety of questions asked by scientists, teachers, and elementary school students about fish: How many fish species are there? Do fish breathe air? What do fish do at night? How long do fish live? Why does a lobster turn red when cooked? The National Marine Fisheries Service, which annually answers thousands of questions like these, has published this clear, informative pamphlet providing over 100 fascinating facts in answer to the most frequently asked questions.

Send: a postcard

Ask for: "Fish: The Most-Asked Questions"

Write to: Public Affairs Office
NOAA
Rockville, MD 20852

School Gardens

School gardens can be living laboratories where teachers involve children in a multitude of experiences. A garden fertilized and tended with natural methods is particularly suited to demonstrating natural cycles and ecological relationships. Learning will be strengthened by involving students in a vital, real-world project, and your schoolyard will be eminently more beautiful. The Sierra Club publishes an 11-page booklet that tells teachers everything they need to know about raising a schoolyard garden.

Send: $1.00

Ask for: "School Gardens"

Write to: Sierra Club
Information Services
730 Polk St.
San Francisco, CA 94109

Hurricane Warning

Through the fictional story of Sue Ellen and her family, kids can relive the devastating experience of hurricane Camille in Mississippi in 1969. NOAA's pamphlet explains how and where hurricanes form, how to track them, and what to do when they strike. There's also a map and an exercise for plotting a hurricane's progress.

Send: a postcard

Ask for: "Hurricane Warning"

Write to: Public Affairs Office
NOAA
Rockville, MD 20852

Trees of Arkansas

The detailed descriptions and line drawings in this unique book will teach students about the many native and ornamental trees of Arkansas. Tips for distinguishing trees by bark, leaves, flowers, fruit, and wood can serve as the basis for fun and educational classroom projects.

Send: $2.00 and purchase order number

Ask for: "Trees of Arkansas," by Dwight M. Moore

Write to: Arkansas Forestry Commission
1 & E Office
P.O. Box 4523
Asher Station
Little Rock, AR 72214

What Should Science Teachers Teach?

Children are very curious about the world in which they live. They are attracted to living things and fascinated by explanations—if the explainer knows how to retain the inherent interest in the phenomenon. In his 45-page paper, Dr. Howard J. Hausman, a member of the Council for Basic Education, describes ways to stimulate a child's curiosity and elaborates on his opinion that science should teach more than just facts and mechanical skills.

Send: $1.00 (plus $2.50 postage & handling)

Ask for: "Choosing a Science Program for the Elementary School"

Write to: Council for Basic Education
725 15th St., N.W.
Washington, DC 20005

Human Anatomy Coloring Book

This 48-page coloring book is an amazing collection of scientifically accurate line drawings of the body's organs and major systems. Cross sections, diagrams, and close-ups are supplemented by informative text. The "Human Anatomy Coloring Book" is the perfect way to introduce anatomy to kids.

Send: $2.50 (plus 85¢ postage & handling)

Ask for: "Human Anatomy Coloring Book"

Write to: Dover Publications, Inc.
31 E. 2nd St.
Mineola, NY 11501

Color a Tree

The beautiful trees of the northeastern United States including the white ash, the red oak, the cottonwood, the sugar maple, and the flowering dogwood are faithfully rendered in this 48-page, 8¼"-by-11" coloring book. Captions accompany each of the 45 drawings, and there are full-color illustrations on the cover.

Send: $2.75 (plus 85¢ postage & handling)

Ask for: "Trees of the Northeast Coloring Book"

Write to: Dover Publications, Inc.
31 E. 2nd St.
Mineola, NY 11501

Science Books Catalog

Dover Publications was a pioneer company in the field of science paperbacks, and in its 64-page catalog, it offers over 300 reasonably priced books covering subjects such as astronomy, physics, mathematics, chemistry, engineering, technology, geology, biology, and popular science.

Send: a postcard

Ask for: science catalog

Write to: Dover Publications, Inc.
31 E. 2nd St.
Mineola, NY 11501

Action Science Experiments

An innovative kit of 23 safe, motivational experiments for 3rd- to 6th-graders, each of which can be completed in 30 to 40 minutes. Using simple equipment commonly found at home and in school, children can try their hand at such terrific experiments as constructing a safety-pin telegraph.

Send: $2.50 (plus $1.00 postage & handling)

Ask for: "Action Science Experiments"

Write to: Teachers Exchange of San Francisco
28 Dawnview
San Francisco, CA 94131

Land Hermit Crab Poster

Printed on both sides, this beautifully illustrated, informative 21-cm.-by-27-cm. poster is perfect for the bulletin board or display. Students will learn where a hermit crab lives, what he eats, and how he moves. Hermit crab activities are listed on the opposite side.

Send: $2.00

Ask for: Land Hermit Crab poster

Write to: National Science Teachers Association
1742 Connecticut Ave., N.W.
Washington, DC 20009

Our Living Oceans

This 6-page pamphlet, written for grade school children, is an ideal first step toward unlocking the magnificent secrets and endless resources of the world's seas and oceans. "Our Living Oceans" gives a basic description of how the sea was first studied, discussing in animated detail the oceans' animal and mineral resources, including fossils and animal favorites such as the whale and octopus. Young readers will also learn how such geological formations as volcanoes affect and change life in the deep sea. This easy-to-understand pamphlet will open a whole new world to children.

Send: a postcard

Ask for: "Our Living Oceans"

Write to: Public Affairs Office
NOAA
Rockville, MD 20852

How Does It Work?

Written for children ages 9 and up, this sensational series of 12 books explains in clear, precise language the basic concepts and mechanics that make things work. The books are full of facts and pictures for the curious child. Series includes "The Motor Car," "The Rocket," "The Aeroplane," "Television," "The Locomotive," "The Hovercraft," "The Camera," "Farm Machinery," "The Computer," "The Telescope and Microscope," "Printing Processes," and "The Telephone."

Send: $2.50 (plus $2.00 postage & handling)

Ask for: desired title

Write to: Ladybird Books, Inc.
Chestnut St.
Lewiston, ME 04240

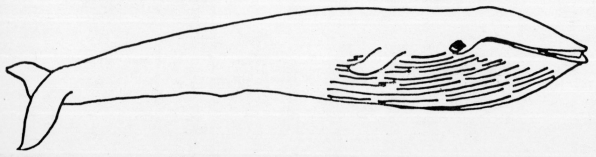

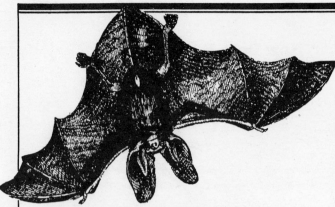

Color a Guppy

There are 41 different species of tropical fish, including the guppy, African knifefish, angelfish, piranha, and many others, as well as 26 species of marine plants, illustrated in this 8¼"-by-11" coloring book. Captions accompany each drawing.

Send: $2.25 (plus 85¢ postage & handling)

Ask for: "Tropical Fish Coloring Book"

Write to: Dover Publications, Inc.
31 E. 2nd St.
Mineola, NY 11501

Get the Facts on Natural History and the Environment

The Massachusetts Audubon Society provides many inexpensive and informative brochures on various aspects of natural history and the environment. The titles include: "How Animals Breathe," "Shore Silhouettes," "Make a Leaf Notebook This Summer," "Care of Amphibians and Reptiles," and "Mosquitoes and Man." The majority of titles are under $1.00.

Send: a postcard

Ask for: Get the Facts catalogs

Write to: Public Information Officer
Massachusetts Audubon
Society
Hatheway Environmental
Resource Center
Lincoln, MA 01773

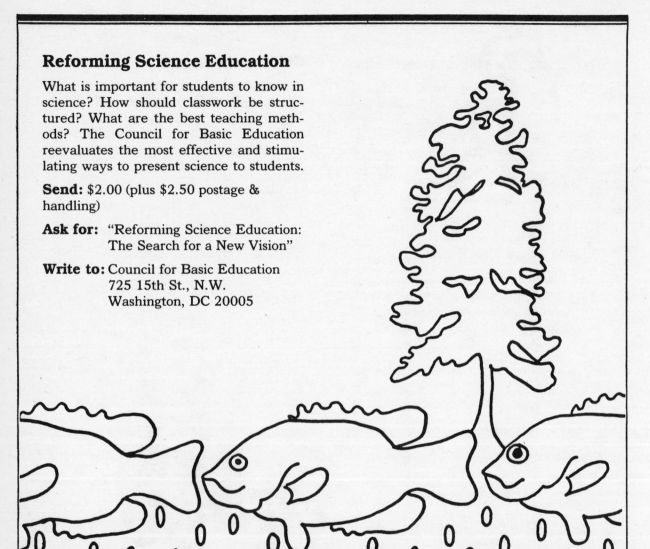

Reforming Science Education

What is important for students to know in science? How should classwork be structured? What are the best teaching methods? The Council for Basic Education reevaluates the most effective and stimulating ways to present science to students.

Send: $2.00 (plus $2.50 postage & handling)

Ask for: "Reforming Science Education: The Search for a New Vision"

Write to: Council for Basic Education
725 15th St., N.W.
Washington, DC 20005

Experiments and Amusements

These 73 simple experiments illustrate a variety of scientific and physics concepts (gravity, sound, vacuums). Science is made simple and fun with unusual projects such as making invisible ink, a pinhole camera, and a mariner's compass. Over 100 photographs and numerous line drawings depict equipment set-up and desired results.

Send: $2.75 (plus 85¢ postage & handling)

Ask for: "Science Experiments and Amusements for Children"

Write to: Dover Publications, Inc.
31 E. 2nd St.
Mineola, NY 11501

Color an Anemone

Identified and illustrated in this 8¼"-by-11" coloring book are 46 scenes of anemones, jellyfish, coral, sea stars, and many other kinds of fish as well as 150 forms of marine life. Examples are shown in color on the cover.

Send: $2.50 (plus 85¢ postage & handling)

Ask for: Seashore Life Coloring Book

Write to: Dover Publications, Inc.
31 E. 2nd St.
Mineola, NY 11501

Windows on Wildlife

The New York Zoological Society publishes a series of six "Windows on Wildlife" booklets suitable for children aged nine through 12. Each of the six—"Grasslands," "Endangered Species," "Rain Forests," "Deciduous Forests," "Wetlands," and "Deserts"—is printed in two colors, is amply illustrated, and contains a glossary and bibliography for students and teachers. This series can form the nucleus of a six-part curriculum on wild animals and their natural habitats.

Send: $1.25 each

Ask for: desired title

Write to: Education Department
New York Zoological Society
Bronx Zoo
Bronx, NY 10460

Solar Fact Sheet

Solar energy is heat and light that comes from the sun. Thousands of years ago some people used this energy to heat their homes. Today, solar energy is again helping to heat buildings.

This five-page fact sheet printed by the Conservation and Renewable Energy Inquiry and Referral Service explains, in elementary language, the whys and hows of solar energy. Diagrams help describe the difference between passive and active collectors and also illustrate various types of heating systems. At the end, 10 questions test your knowledge. An easy way to learn the basics of solar energy.

Send: a postcard

Ask for: "Solar Fact Sheet"

Write to: Conservation and Renewable
Energy Inquiry and Referral
Service
P.O. Box 8900
Silver Spring, MD 20850

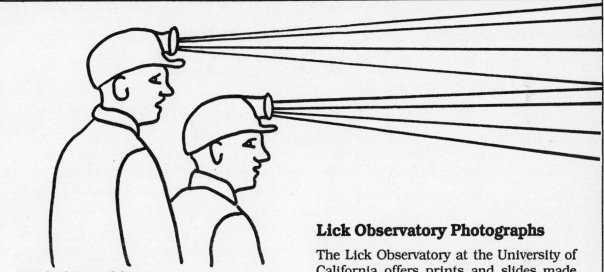

Buried Sunshine

This 19-page, two-color booklet titled "The Power of Coal" describes the beginnings, history, production, and uses of bituminous coal. A teacher's guide and student quizzes are included. Suitable for grades one through six.

Send: a postcard

Ask for: "The Power of Coal"

Write to: American Coal Foundation
918 16th St., N.W.
Suite 404
Washington, DC 20006

Lick Observatory Photographs

The Lick Observatory at the University of California offers prints and slides made from astronomical photographs taken with its telescopes. The photographs are available in three standard formats: 35-mm. slides in 2"-by-2" cardboard mounts, 8"-by-10" glossy prints, and 14"-by-17" glossy paper, dried-matte prints. The catalog shows a photograph of every print or slide available. California residents must add 6.5% tax.

Send: 50¢

Ask for: astronomical photographs catalog

Write to: Lick Observatory OP
University of California
Santa Cruz, CA 95064

XIV. Social Studies

Bicentennial of the U.S. Constitution

The Commission on the Bicentennial of the United States Constitution has included a wide variety of special educational programs among its plans to celebrate the 200th anniversary of the signing of the U.S. Constitution on September 17, 1787, and of the Bill of Rights on December 15, 1791. Students will delight in learning from free pocket-size copies of the Constitution. And bicentennial calendars—with day-by-day historical information on events that led to the signings—will also be available in 1987 and 1988. A perfect way to learn about the history of our unique legal system.

Send: a postcard

Ask for: pocket-size Constitution and free calendar

Write to: Commission on the Bicentennial of the United States Constitution
736 Jackson Pl., N.W.
Washington, DC 20503

Definitions of Racism

This 4-page pamphlet defines racism, describing the many obvious and subtle ways racism is manifest in American society. Complete with clear examples and explanations of the difference between racism and prejudice, this important publication provides vital eye-opening facts for kids and teachers. Set of 10 pamphlets.

Send: $1.00

Ask for: "Definitions of Racism"

Write to: Council on Interracial Books
CIBC Resource Center
1841 Broadway
New York, NY 10023

What Is a Dollar?

This pamphlet published by the Federal Reserve Bank of Boston takes a close look at the one dollar bill and at other types of U.S. currency. It explains how paper money was first created, what all those little numbers and codes really mean, and the value of the dollar as a medium of exchange. Students will also learn which president's portrait appears on which bill and other bits of trivia about U.S. currency.

What Is China All About?

China Books & Periodicals, the national importer of publications from China, offers a wide range of educational materials. Children's books, maps, posters, dictionaries, histories, novels, fairy tales, picture books, art prints, and note cards are only a few of the items offered. Write for their free catalog and welcome China into your classroom.

Send: a postcard

Ask for: catalog

Write to: China Books & Periodicals, Inc.
2929 24th St.
San Francisco, CA 94110

Send: a postcard

Ask for: "Dollar Points"

Write to: Publications Dept.
Federal Reserve Bank of
Boston
600 Atlantic Ave.
Boston, MA 02106

The Quakers

The Quakers were one of the first religious groups in America, and their story is both fascinating and unusual. From the mid-17th century to the present, this informative booklet traces the history of the Quakers in America. Details on modern-day Quaker institutions, beliefs, and life-style will acquaint children with an American way of life that may be very different from their own.

Send: $2.00 (plus $1.00 postage & handling)

Ask for: "The Quakers" (item no. 0904)

Write to: Publications Sales Program
Friends of the Pennsylvania
Historical and Museum
Commission
P.O. Box 11466
Harrisburg, PA 17108

Folk Costumes of Europe

Authentic costumes—130 of them—from Italy, Spain, Russia, Central Europe, the Balkans, and many other areas are accurately illustrated in this 48-page coloring book. Captions accompany each illustration.

Send: $2.75 (plus 85¢ postage & handling)

Ask for: "Folk Costumes of Europe Coloring Book"

Write to: Dover Publications, Inc.
31 E. 2nd St.
Mineola, NY 11501

Learn About New Zealand

If you are planning a study unit on New Zealand, the Information Office of the New Zealand Embassy in Washington will send you an information package that includes a New Zealand information map; a beautifully illustrated 49-page booklet on the land, its history, and its people; a red, white, and blue paper copy of the national flag; and a list of films about New Zealand available for loan from the Modern Talking Picture Service. Well worthwhile for anyone interested in this nation of islands. Single copies only.

Send: a postcard

Ask for: teacher's information package

Write to: Information Office
New Zealand Embassy
37 Observatory Circle, N.W.
Washington, DC 20008

Model UN Kit

In 1945, the peoples of the United Nations resolved to practice tolerance and live together in peace with one another, to unite our strength, to maintain international peace and security, to ensure that armed force would not be used except in the common interest, and to employ machinery for the promotion of the economic and social advancement of all peoples. The model UN kit contains information on the work of the UN and describes how resolutions are passed. It also provides information for schools that would like to participate in the model UN program. One kit per school.

Send: request on school letterhead

Ask for: Model UN Kit

Write to: United Nations Public Inquiries
Unit
Room GA-57
United Nations, NY 10017

Yorktown

Relive the excitement of the Revolutionary War period using the materials and activities included in this teacher's kit. Students can follow historical events and the progress of the Revolutionary War on a map provided for that purpose.

Send: $2.00

Ask for: "Yorktown"—teacher's kit

Write to: Education Department
Jamestown-Yorktown
Foundation
Drawer JF
Williamsburg, VA 23187

The Arabian Peninsula

Americans for Middle East Understanding will provide teachers with a color wall map, 29½"-by-21", of the Arabian peninsula. Printed on heavy stock, this handsome map marks major cities along the Persian Gulf and the Red Sea and indicates mountains, deserts, cultivated areas, and major roads. Both mile and kilometer measurements are given, and an insert shows where the peninsula is in relation to Europe, Asia, India, and Africa.

Send: 50¢

Ask for: map of the Arabian peninsula

Write to: Americans for Middle East
Understanding, Inc.
475 Riverside Dr., Room 771
New York, NY 10027

Color Airplanes of the Second World War

Douglas SBD Dauntless, 1941. Already outdated at the time of the Japanese attack on Pearl Harbor, the Dauntless nevertheless bore the brunt of aerial warfare in the Pacific until more sophisticated aircraft arrived.

This informative coloring book includes 46 drawings of fighters, bombers, reconnaissance planes, and transports that were used by every country involved in World War II. Detailed captions offer information about markings, insignias, design innovations, and each plane's military role and affiliation.

Send: $2.50 (plus 85¢ postage and handling)

Ask for: "Airplanes of the Second World War"

Write to: Dover Publications, Inc.
31 E. 2nd St.
Mineola, NY 11501

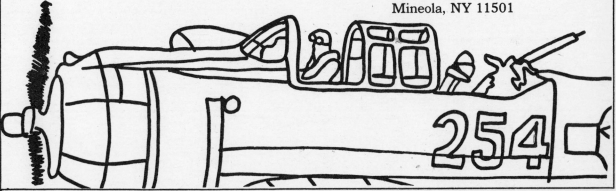

Historic Pennsylvania

The Pennsylvania Historical and Museum Commission publishes a number of fascinating books and pamphlets covering every aspect of Pennsylvania's history. Its list of books and publications is categorized by subject; some of the areas covered are the tercentenary, native Americans, the fight for independence, industry and work, culture and art, historical preservation, and Pennsylvania at war. A valuable resource for any teacher interested in teaching about our roots.

Send: a postcard

Ask for: "Books and Publications"

Write to: Publications Sales Program
Friends of the Pennsylvania
Historical and Museum
Commission
P.O. Box 11466
Harrisburg, PA 17108

Biography of Helen Keller

This 8-page pamphlet published by the American Foundation for the Blind describes the life of this extraordinary writer, who spent her adulthood working to help those less fortunate than herself. The pamphlet is filled with photographs of Keller with Charlie Chaplin, Alexander Graham Bell, and other goodwill emissaries. Great inspirational material.

Send: 35¢

Ask for: "Helen Keller" (FISO33)

Write to: American Foundation for the
Blind
15 W. 16th St.
New York, NY 10011

Grass Roots Preservation

Teach your students to preserve their history! The Champaign County Historical Museum of Champaign, Illinois, publishes a 24-page booklet that describes ways local historical organizations and school personnel can work together to develop preservation-related projects to supplement the social studies curriculum. The booklet is filled with photographs and a resource list is included.

Send: $1.90

Ask for: "Grass Roots Preservation"

Write to: Champaign County Historical
Museum
709 W. University Ave.
Champaign, IL 61820

Turkish Delights

Topkapi Palace in Istanbul, Homer's Troy on the Aegean, Ataturk's Mausoleum in Ankara, and the breathtaking landscapes of the Black Sea Coast are just a few examples of this magical Mideastern country. The Turkish Embassy offers four brochures illustrating in full color other highlights.

Send: a postcard

Ask for: brochures on Turkey

Write to: Turkish Embassy
Office of the Tourism and
Information Counselor
821 United Nations Plaza
New York, NY 10017

Teaching About Native Americans

Dover publishes an excellent 91-page ethnobiography of the Winnebago Indian during the late 19th and early 20th centuries. In it, Paul Radin describes tribal life, acculturation, peyote, the loss of values, and other aspects of the Winnebago culture.

Send: $2.25 (plus 85¢ postage and handling)

Ask for: "The Autobiography of a Winnebago Indian"

Write to: Dover Publications, Inc.
31 E. 2nd St.
Mineola, NY 11501

From Geography to Politics

Numerous inexpensive publications on everything from different countries and people to governments and historical personalities are to be found among the multitude of educational books and pamphlets published by Troll Associates. Teachers will find numerous popular materials to supplement any social studies topic—indeed, just about any topic at all.

Send: request on school letterhead

Ask for: elementary paperback catalog

Write to: Troll Associates
320 Route 17
Mahwah, NJ 07430

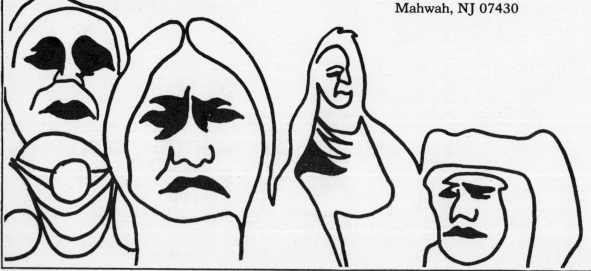

Chinese Legends and Tales

The fabulous images of dragons and numerous other animals, plants, and people recur again and again in Chinese art and culture. The age-old tales and legends from which these images are drawn are recounted for readers in rich detail in this fully illustrated book which will add enormously to your understanding of Chinese culture.

Send: $1.95

Ask for: "Legends and Tales from History" (no. 1618-2)

Write to: China Books & Periodicals, Inc.
2929 24th St.
San Francisco, CA 94110

Pennsylvania Heritage

In this read-and-color book on historic Pennsylvania, your students will learn about William Penn, Daniel Boone, Joseph Priestly, the flagship *Niagara*, the Battle of Gettysburg, and many other important events that helped make Penn's land the Bicentennial State. A colorful way to learn American history.

Send: 50¢

Ask for: "Pennsylvania Heritage: A Read and Color Book"

Write to: Publications Sales Program
Friends of the Pennsylvania
Historical and Museum
Commission
P.O. Box 11466
Harrisburg, PA 17108

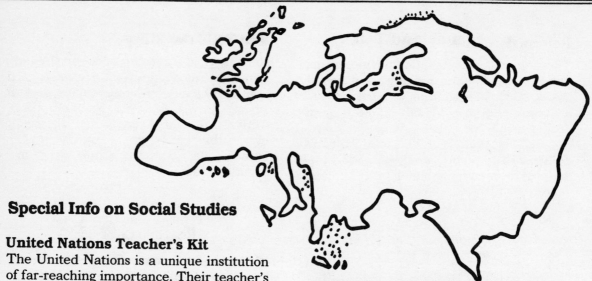

Special Info on Social Studies

United Nations Teacher's Kit

The United Nations is a unique institution of far-reaching importance. Their teacher's kit is of exceptional value, as it contains not only information on the workings of the UN itself, but also supplies details on how additional educational materials on many topical issues and world concerns can be obtained from various agencies and programs of the UN.

Send: a postcard

Ask for: Teacher's Kit

Write to: United Nations Public Inquiries
Unit
Room GA-57
United Nations
New York, NY 10017

The Heart of Europe

The Austrian Press and Information Service will provide you with a full-color guide to the Republic of Austria. Besides the usual statistical data, the brochure explains Austria's economic system, culture, and government. A brief history, map, and many photographs are included.

Send: a postcard

Ask for: "Austria at the Heart of Europe"

Write to: Austrian Press and Information
Service
31 E. 69th St.
New York, NY 10021

Colombia: Land of Contrasts

The Colombian Information Service offers four ready reference materials on the land that was conquered by Spaniards in the 15th century and set free by Simón Bolívar in the 19th century. Illustrated with line drawings, "Columbia, A Land of Contrasts" includes basic facts about the country's history, government, transportation, education, agriculture, major cities, and art, music, and literature. "A Sketch of Colombia" is filled with photographs and describes the land and its people. "Quick Facts About Colombia" lists basic data such as population, labor force, natural resources, and exports and imports. "The Story of Colombian Coffee" describes the history of Colombia's major crop, how it is cultivated, and its importance in the world coffee market.

Send: a postcard

Ask for: the brochure by name

Write to: Publications Director
Columbia Information Service
140 E. 57th St.
New York, NY 10022

Tea Tells the Story

What better way to teach your students about Japanese culture than by explaining the ancient and elegant art of a ritual tea ceremony? Kakuzo Okakura's minor classic presents an entertaining and charming explanation of Oriental culture in terms of the tea ceremony. There are 94 5⅜"-by-8½" pages.

Send: $2.50 (plus 85¢ postage & handling)

Ask for: "The Book of Tea"

Write to: Dover Publications, Inc.
31 E. 2nd St.
Mineola, NY 11501

A Visit to Ancient Egypt

Jump back to the age of Cleopatra, King Tut, and the Egyptian pyramids with this set of 66 prints. The colorful pictures illustrate the well-known people and sites of the era, as well as scenes depicting religion, art, crafts, and day-to-day life-styles of ancient Egyptians.

Send: $3.00 (plus $1.00 postage & handling)

Ask for: "A Visit to Ancient Egypt"

Write to: The University Prints
21 East St.
P.O. Box 485
Winchester, PA 01890

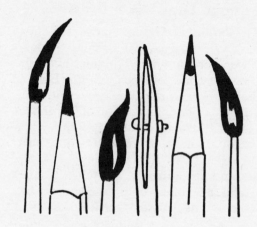

Color the Civil War

In this coloring book, 24 Confederate and 24 Union uniforms of every rank, state, and unit are accurately illustrated, as are historical figures including Grant, Lee, and Farragut. Informative captions accompany each illustration.

Send: $2.75 (plus 85¢ postage & handling)

Ask for: "Civil War Uniforms Coloring Book"

Write to: Dover Publications, Inc.
31 E. 2nd St.
Mineola, NY 11501

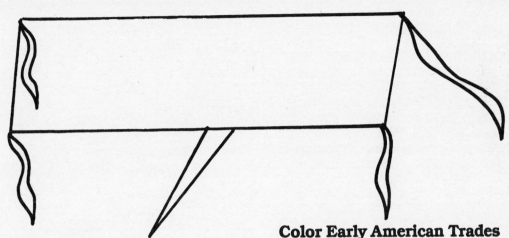

Space Stamps

This colorful collection of 100 different stamps from around the world celebrates the continued marvel of space exploration.

Send: $2.00

Ask for: "Space Stamps"

Write to: Space Stamps
P.O. Box 466C
Port Washington, NY 11050

Color Early American Trades

This valuable coloring book shows wig-makers, farriers, glassblowers, hatters, whitesmiths, cutlers, coopers, cabinet-makers, coppersmiths, and 13 other tradesmen at work in period costumes. Illustrations of tools and products associated with each trade are on facing pages. This 48-page book has 44 plates and 22 captions.

Send: $2.00 (plus 85¢ postage & handling)

Ask for: "Early American Trades Coloring Book"

Write to: Dover Publications, Inc.
31 E. 2nd St.
Mineola, NY 11501

How Are Shoes Made?

The Brown Shoe Co. offers a student kit titled "A Study of Shoemaking." This collection of educational materials includes information on the history of shoes, the art of making a shoe, and a 23-page booklet titled "Your Feet Were Made for Walking." What better way to teach the integration of mind and body than with a discussion of the toe and its covering. Limit one per teacher.

Send: a postcard

Ask for: "A Study in Shoemaking"

Write to: Brown Shoe Co.
Student Kit
8300 Maryland, P.O. Box 354
St. Louis, MO 63166

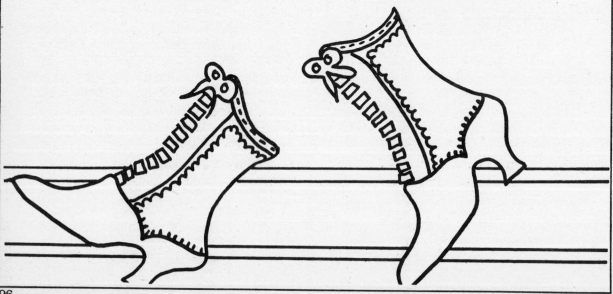

The FBI on the FBI

How many fingerprints does the FBI have on file? How does a criminal make it to the Ten Most Wanted list? What steps does the FBI take to counter terrorism? These and other questions on structure, jurisdiction, and methods of criminal investigation are answered in the 30-page booklet, "99 Facts about the FBI." A second booklet, "The FBI: The First 75 Years," chronicles the evolution of the bureau from its creation by Theodore Roosevelt in 1908 to the present.

Send: a postcard

Ask for: booklet by name

Write to: Publications
FBI Headquarters
U.S. Dept. of Justice
Washington, DC 20535

How Money and Stamps Are Made

The Bureau of Engraving and Printing is the world's largest securities manufacturing establishment. It designs, engraves, and prints U.S. paper currency; Treasury bonds, bills, notes, and certificates of indebtedness; U.S. postage and revenue stamps; and over 800 miscellaneous items for various departments and agencies in the federal government. The operations of the bureau, including an examination of how currency and postage stamps are made, are offered in their free flier.

Send: a postcard

Ask for: "Production of Government Securities"

Write to: Public Affairs Dept.
Dept. of the Treasury
Bureau of Engraving and
Printing
Washington, DC 20228

Color the American Revolution

The entire panorama of military attire from the American battle for independence is reproduced in 31 lively drawings. Each uniform has complete instructions for accurate coloring.

Send: $2.75 (plus 85¢ postage & handling)

Ask for: "Uniforms of the American Revolution Coloring Book"

Write to: Dover Publications
31 E. 2nd St.
Mineola, NY 11501

Peace, War, and the Nuclear Threat

Some children start playing war games at a very early age—for example, learning to hit one another to solve problems. The National Association for the Education of Young Children believes in educating young children about the worldwide threat of war and nuclear arms. Toward that end, this book is designed to help adults instill in children a desire to seek peaceful solutions to problems.

Send: $3.00

Ask for: "Helping Young Children Understand Peace, War, and the Nuclear Threat" (NAEYC #321)

Write to: National Association for the Education of Young Children
1834 Connecticut Ave., N.W.
Washington, DC 20009

Vintage U.S. Coins

The design of American coins and the metal used to make them have changed significantly since the first U.S. coins were pounded out of pieces of silver and gold. The many different kinds of vintage American coins serve as a beautiful and fascinating testimony to the evolution and changes in American currency and American history. For just one dollar, Joan Alexander will send you two Buffalo nickels and a Lincoln Head cent dated 1936 or earlier. This is a fabulous bargain for collectors and an interesting memento of America's past.

Send: $1.00

Ask for: "Buffalo Nickels and Lincoln Head Cent"

Write to: Joan Alexander
P.O. Box 7N
Roslyn, NY 11576

Color a Broomseller

In this coloring book, a farmer, wagoner, sailor, cooper, broomseller, and 41 other characters from the Colonial period in America are accurately illustrated. Each is accompanied by captions, and 14 examples are shown in color on the cover.

Send: $2.75 (plus 85¢ postage & handling)

Ask for: "Everyday Dress of the American Colonial Period Coloring Book"

Write to: Dover Publications, Inc.
31 E. 2nd St.
Mineola, NY 11501

XV. Special Children

Reliable Information on Dyslexia

The Public Affairs Committee offers a concise pamphlet, written by a specialist in medical issues, on learning disabilities and the possible causes. The booklet describes various ways of detecting problems, methods of prevention and treatment, and ways that parents and teachers can help. A bibliography and a list of organizations are included.

Send: $1.00

Ask for: pamphlet no. 578

Write to: Dept. FTT
Public Affairs Pamphlets
Public Affairs Committee, Inc.
381 Park Ave. South
New York, NY 10016

Early Warning Signs

Some children are born with physical or mental conditions—or they may acquire disorders that handicap normal growth and development. Fortunately, many of these conditions can be corrected if parents and teachers recognize the problem early and seek help. A pamphlet published by The National Easter Seal Society lists some of the early warning signs and some of the more common indications that a problem may exist. They also list people and organizations that can help.

Send: 50¢

Ask for: "Are You Listening to What Your Child May Not Be Saying?"

Write to: The National Easter Seal Society
2023 W. Ogden Ave.
Chicago, IL 60612

Stuttering Words

The Speech Foundation of America has published an authoritative glossary of the meanings of the words and terms used or associated with the field of stuttering, speech pathology, and its treatment. A unique and educational guide.

Send: 50¢ (plus $1.00 postage & handling)

Ask for: "Stuttering Words, Publication No. 2"

Write to: Speech Foundation of America
P.O. Box 11749
Memphis, TN 38111

For the Learning Disabled

The ninth edition of the "Directory of Facilities and Services for Learning Disabled" lists hundreds of organizations in the U.S. and Canada of help to the parents and teachers of learning-disabled students. The name, address, telephone number, and information on staff is included for each facility listed.

Send: $1.50

Ask for: "Directory of Facilities and Services for Learning Disabled"

Write to: Academic Therapy Publications
20 Commercial Blvd.
Novato, CA 94947

Helping the Gifted Child

"He is the kind of child a teacher dreams of having once in a lifetime. But now that we have him, we don't know what to do with him." How many teachers have uttered the same words as this teacher of a fifth-grader who was blessed with an IQ of 169? More often than not, to be a gifted child in a school is to be a handicapped child, but Drs. James Gallagher and Patricia Weiss are trying to remedy the problem. In their booklet, these educators explain what giftedness means and detail the emerging opportunites for the education of the gifted and specially talented student.

Send: $2.00 (plus $2.50 postage & handling)

Ask for: "The Education of Gifted and Talented Students"

Write to: Council for Basic Education
725 15th St., N.W.
Washington, DC 20005

When You Have a Visually Handicapped Child in Your Classroom

This 28-page handbook lists practical suggestions for the teacher who has a visually handicapped student in the regular classroom. It includes advice about attitudes, mobility, materials, resources, personnel, and information about special devices. A bibliography and organizations list is also included.

Send: 35¢

Ask for: "When You Have a Visually Handicapped Child in Your Classroom" (FEL057)

Write to: American Foundation for the Blind
15 W. 16th St.
New York, NY 10011

Disabling Myths About Disability

Without realizing it, we often perpetuate myths about disability, and these habitual ways of thinking can hinder full human expression. Teachers especially should examine their attitudes and work to counteract any that might be harmful to students. In this pamphlet published by the National Easter Seal Society, Bernice A. Wright, professor of psychology at the University of Kansas, examines the myths and the mischief they create.

Send: $1.00

Ask for: "Disabling Myths About Disability"

Write to: The National Easter Seal Society
2023 W. Ogden Ave.
Chicago, IL 60612

XVI. Sports, Games, and Hobbies

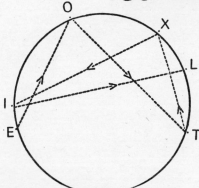

Beginner's Compass Game

The Beginner's Compass Game is an exciting way to learn proper compass usage. The game is easy to set up and requires little space or equipment. Plans for 90 different games are included.

Send: $1.50

Ask for: Beginner's Compass Game

Write to: Orienteering Services, U.S.A.
P.O. Box 1604
Binghamton, NY 13902

Roller Skates

In the past few years, roller skating has become one of the most popular sports in America. The Chicago Roller Skate Co. offers two booklets that include information on skating skills and safety. Both are illustrated and easy to read.

Send: 50¢ plus self-addressed, stamped envelope

Ask for: "How to Roller Skate" and "Skating Skills"

Write to: Chicago Roller Skate Co.
4458 W. Lake St.
Chicago, IL 60624

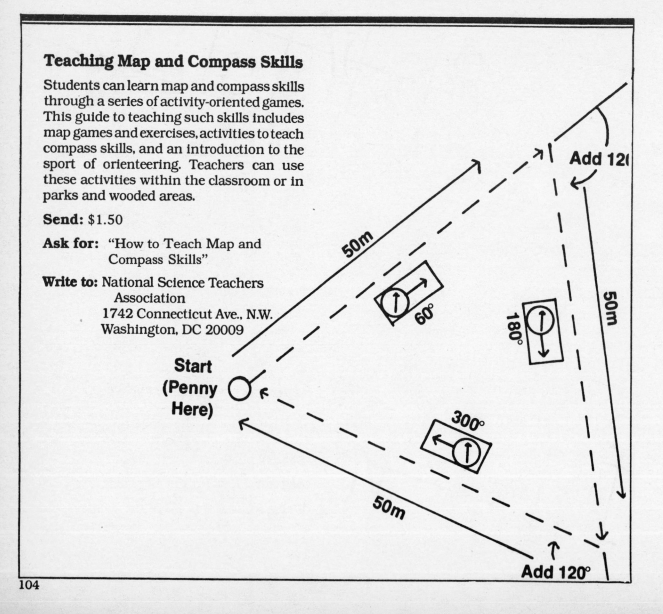

Teaching Map and Compass Skills

Students can learn map and compass skills through a series of activity-oriented games. This guide to teaching such skills includes map games and exercises, activities to teach compass skills, and an introduction to the sport of orienteering. Teachers can use these activities within the classroom or in parks and wooded areas.

Send: $1.50

Ask for: "How to Teach Map and Compass Skills"

Write to: National Science Teachers Association
1742 Connecticut Ave., N.W.
Washington, DC 20009

How Do You Play Chess?

In this complete, 32-page beginner's guide to chess, Fred Reinfeld presents the basic rules with utmost clarity. The author answers 73 commonly asked questions and offers a list of recommended reading.

Send: a postcard

Ask for: "How Do You Play Chess?"

Write to: Dover Publications, Inc.
         31 E. 2nd St.
         Mineola, NY 11501

Everyone Loves a Pen Pal

Having pen pals can be great fun for children. They can write to their far-away friends about all the things they like to do: play tennis, draw, skateboard—whatever! Children interested in corresponding with pen pals can "meet" boys and girls ages 7–11 and 12–15. Each child receives three names and addresses plus a high quality ballpoint pen.

Send: $1.00 (plus name, complete address, and age)

Ask for: "Perfect Pen Pals"

Write to: Perfect Pen Pals
P.O. Box 7154
Hicksville, NY 11801

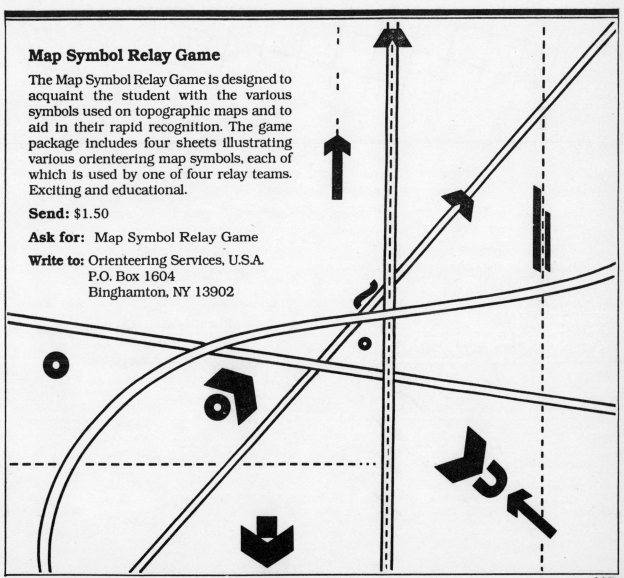

Map Symbol Relay Game

The Map Symbol Relay Game is designed to acquaint the student with the various symbols used on topographic maps and to aid in their rapid recognition. The game package includes four sheets illustrating various orienteering map symbols, each of which is used by one of four relay teams. Exciting and educational.

Send: $1.50

Ask for: Map Symbol Relay Game

Write to: Orienteering Services, U.S.A.
P.O. Box 1604
Binghamton, NY 13902

Let's Play Ball

Basketball, volleyball, and kickball are three all-time favorites with kids. "Let's Play Ball," designed by an experienced elementary school P.E. teacher, is a step-by-step program that will aid in creating an effective physical education program for developing coordination and skills in these sports.

Send: $1.95 (plus $1.00 postage & handling)

Ask for: "Let's Play Ball"

Write to: Teachers Exchange of San Francisco
28 Dawnview
San Francisco, CA 94131

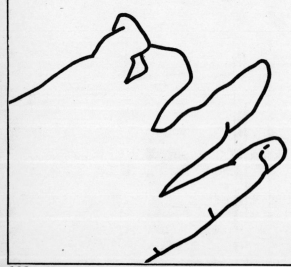

Official Floor and Poly Hockey Rulebook

In this handy guidebook to one of the fastest-growing sports in America, Cosom tells the history and fundamentals of floor hockey, rules, techniques of play, rules for poly hockey, and guidelines for wheelchair hockey. A score sheet and list of equipment are included. Amply illustrated with black-and-white photographs.

Send: $1.00

Ask for: "Official Rulebook for Floor
Hockey and Poly Hockey"

Write to: Cosom
9909 South Shore Dr.
P.O. Box 1426
Minneapolis, MN 55440

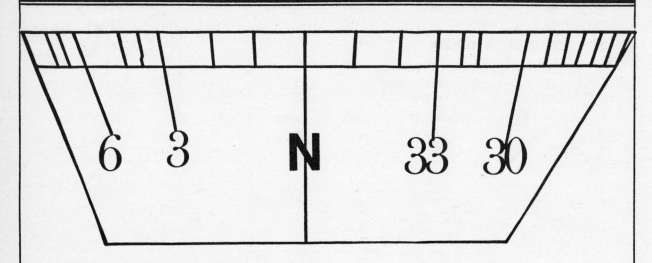

Metric Compass Game

The Metric Compass Game is designed to assist teachers in imparting the basic compass skills of setting bearings and pacing to specific locations. The game is fun and competitive and provides compass training without elaborate preparation. The 25 separate trails, each having three directions of travel, are automatically established by setting out a row of stakes.

Send: $1.50

Ask for: Compass Game

Write to: Orienteering Services, U.S.A.
P.O. Box 1604
Binghamton, NY 13902

Mazes and Labyrinths

This unusual 122-page book offers 50 amusements using the principle of the maze. It includes classic mazes, 3-D mazes, Moebius-strip mazes, and hidden messages. Most are based on story situations. Great for students of any age.

Send: $2.95 (plus 85¢ postage & handling)

Ask for: "Mazes and Labyrinths: A Book of Puzzles"

Write to: Dover Publications, Inc.
31 E. 2nd St.
Mineola, NY 11501

The Importance of Play

An educator who plays with children may rediscover his or her own creative responses and the pleasure of moving expressively. Montessori educators believe that play and creative interaction are important parts of a child's education—play can be a significant way of expressing the joy of being oneself. Guidelines for encouraging the child to discover the dance from within are offered in a booklet published by the American Montessori Society.

Send: $1.00

Ask for: X108 "Play Behaviors of Young Children"

Write to: American Montessori Society
150 Fifth Ave.
New York, NY 10011

FDR Philatelic Society

Stamp collecting can be an exciting and instructive hobby. The Franklin D. Roosevelt Philatelic Society, an international association of collectors of postage stamps issued to honor Franklin D. Roosevelt, offers ten Roosevelt stamps and two cacheted special events covers to teachers who would like to introduce this historic philatelic hobby to their students. Collectors are welcome to join the society.

Send: $3.00

Ask for: ten Roosevelt stamps and two cacheted covers

Write to: Gustav Detjen, Jr., President
The FDR Philatelic Society
154 Laguna Court
St. Augustine Shores, FL
32086

Secret Codes

The editor of *The Shadow* magazine has put together a 117-page book of over 50 codes and secret methods used by cryptographers. This imaginative book is written for the elementary student and stresses substitution. Terrific mental exercise.

Send: $2.50 (plus 85¢ postage & handling)

Ask for: "Secret Writing"

Write to: Dover Publications, Inc.
31 E. 2nd St.
Mineola, NY 11501

Beginner's Stamp Album

This attractive album has spaces for over 2500 stamps from nearly 200 different countries. Complete with tips on obtaining, handling, and mounting stamps, "A First Stamp Album" is the perfect introduction to the varied world of stamp collecting.

Send: $2.95 (plus 85¢ postage & handling)

Ask for: "A First Stamp Album for Beginners"

Write to: Dover Publications, Inc.
31 E. 2nd St.
Mineola, NY 11501

Let's Play Scoop

In its illustrated guide to scoop games, Cosom details the fundamentals of scoop and fun ball, and outlines 11 games for beginners and 15 games for advanced players. The diagrams are clear, the instructions explicit.

Send: 75¢

Ask for: "Scoop Book"

Write to: Cosom
9909 South Shore Dr.
P.O. Box 1426
Minneapolis, MN 55440

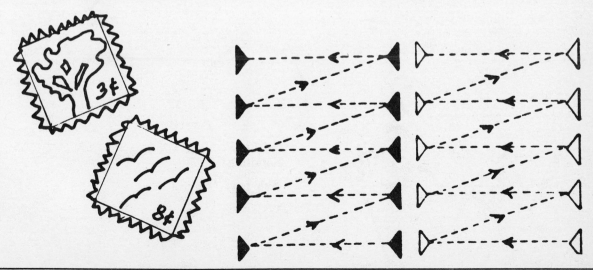

Official Handball and Racquetball Rules

Handball and racquetball are rapidly gaining popularity, and the Champion Glove Manufacturing Co. will supply you with an authoritative guide to the official rules of both games. This booklet details the nature of the game, the required facilities and equipment. It describes the uniform and game officials and defines the terms and game-playing regulations. The book to have if you want to teach the sport correctly.

Send: $1.00

Ask for: "Official Handball Rules/Official Racquetball Rules"

Write to: Champion Glove Mfg. Co.
2200 E. Ovid
Des Moines, IA 50313

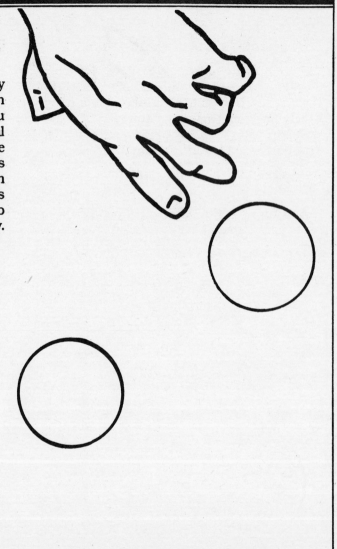
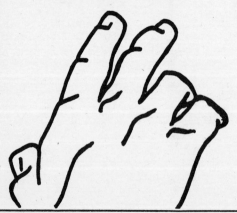

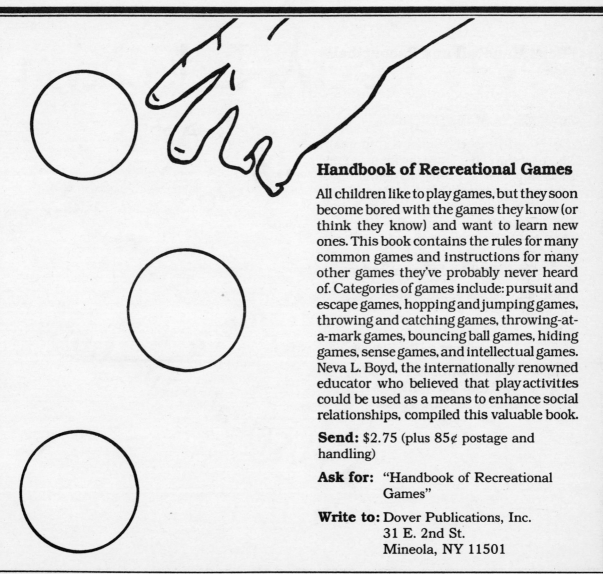

Handbook of Recreational Games

All children like to play games, but they soon become bored with the games they know (or think they know) and want to learn new ones. This book contains the rules for many common games and instructions for many other games they've probably never heard of. Categories of games include: pursuit and escape games, hopping and jumping games, throwing and catching games, throwing-at-a-mark games, bouncing ball games, hiding games, sense games, and intellectual games. Neva L. Boyd, the internationally renowned educator who believed that play activities could be used as a means to enhance social relationships, compiled this valuable book.

Send: $2.75 (plus 85¢ postage and handling)

Ask for: "Handbook of Recreational Games"

Write to: Dover Publications, Inc.
31 E. 2nd St.
Mineola, NY 11501

XVII. Teacher Education

Curriculum Management

The conditions that make important differences in schools are the instructional leadership of the principal, definition of purpose, expectations of students, and time spent "on task." In his 26-page paper, Fenwick English describes the strenuous measures he feels are required to improve school curriculum. English is a former teacher, principal, and superintendent.

Send: $2.00 (plus $2.50 postage & handling)

Ask for: "Improving Curriculum Management in the Schools"

Write to: Council for Basic Education
725 15th St., N.W.
Washington, DC 20005

Art

Music

Mathematics

Science

Physical education

History

English

Health

The Montessori Alternative

A child's world is full of sights and sounds that at first appear chaotic. From this chaos, the child gradually creates order and learns to distinguish among the impressions that assail his or her senses, slowly gaining mastery of self and environment. Maria Montessori developed what she called "the prepared environment" for the education of children. Among its features is an ordered arrangement of learning materials in a noncompetitive atmosphere that enhances a child's ability to grow at his or her own rate. The Montessori method in its American form is described in a booklet published by the American Montessori Society.

Send: 50¢

Ask for: XO39 "Montessori as an American Public School Alternative"

Write to: American Montessori Society
150 Fifth Ave.
New York, NY 10011

Teachers and A.A.

Alcoholics Anonymous, the reputable fellowship of men and women who believe that alcoholism is a disease that can be controlled, publishes a number of booklets of interest to educators. "A Brief Guide to Alcoholics Anonymous" defines the disease, explains the nature of the organization, and tells where to find more information. If you think you might have a problem, or suspect that one of your students might, this is a welcome and instructive pamphlet.

Send: 10¢

Ask for: P-42

Write to: A.A. World Services, Inc.
P.O. Box 459
Grand Central Station
New York, NY 10163

Burnout

Burnout is defined as physical, emotional, and attitudinal exhaustion. It may show up as low staff morale, frequent absenteeism, or high job turnover. Teachers are particularly prone to burnout; indeed, some fear that burnout has reached epidemic proportions. ERIC offers a fact sheet that discusses the ailment and cites possible personal and institutional remedies.

Send: a postcard

Ask for: Fact Sheet Number 3

Write to: ERIC Clearinghouse on
Urban Education
Box 40
Teachers College
Columbia University
New York, NY 10027

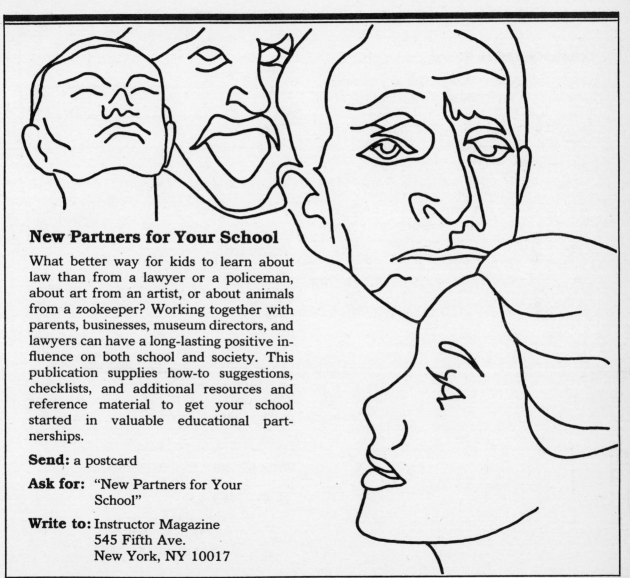

New Partners for Your School

What better way for kids to learn about law than from a lawyer or a policeman, about art from an artist, or about animals from a zookeeper? Working together with parents, businesses, museum directors, and lawyers can have a long-lasting positive influence on both school and society. This publication supplies how-to suggestions, checklists, and additional resources and reference material to get your school started in valuable educational partnerships.

Send: a postcard

Ask for: "New Partners for Your School"

Write to: Instructor Magazine
545 Fifth Ave.
New York, NY 10017

What Are Other Teachers Saying?

The Institute for Research on Teaching publishes "Communication Quarterly," an informative bulletin that covers subjects of interest to today's teachers. The IRT is funded by a variety of sources, including the U.S. Department of Education and Michigan State University, and is based at the College of Education at Michigan State University. Recent articles have covered methods of motivating students, teaching science, and improving reading and writing skills. Important for any teacher who wants to keep up to date.

Send: a postcard

Ask for: sample of "Communication Quarterly"

Write to: Editor
Institute for Research on Teaching
252 Erickson, MSU
East Lansing, MI 48824

Uses and Abuses of Standardized Tests

On the whole, reading readiness tests and the approach of which they are a part do more harm than good. It would be wiser to begin formal reading instruction, as some schools do, by attempting to teach all children the same things, without prejudging or predicting their success. These ideas and others are elaborated in a booklet written by George Weber, associate director for the Council for Basic Education.

Send: $1.00

Ask for: "Uses and Abuses of Standardized Testing in the Schools"

Write to: Council for Basic Education
725 15th St., N.W.
Washington, DC 20005

Submit Your Paper to ERIC

The staff of ERIC, the Educational Resources Information Center, invites you to submit your document to their clearinghouse. If accepted, the document will become part of a permanent collection in microfiche and will be available in over 650 libraries and other facilities throughout the world. ERIC is interested in documents relevant to urban life and schooling; the education of urban minorities; the performance of urban children; the effects of urban experiences on children and adults; economic and ethnic discrimination, segregation, and integration; and many other areas. This brochure provides full information.

Send: a postcard

Ask for: "ERIC/CUE Invites You to Submit Your Documents to ERIC"

Write to: ERIC Clearinghouse on Urban Education
Box 40
Teachers College
Columbia University
New York, NY 10027

Racism in Our Language

Language is an integral part of any culture. It not only develops in conjunction with a society's historical, economic, and political evolution, but also reflects the society's attitudes and thinking. It not only expresses ideas and concepts, but actually shapes thoughts. If one accepts that our dominant white culture is racist, then one would expect our language to be racist as well. In this essay published by the Council on Interracial Books, the author describes the ways our language transmits racist concepts and outlines five lesson plans for detecting racist language and practicing nonracist language.

Send: $2.50

Ask for: "Racism in the English Language"

Write to: The Council on Interracial Books
CIBC Resource Center
1841 Broadway
New York, NY 10023

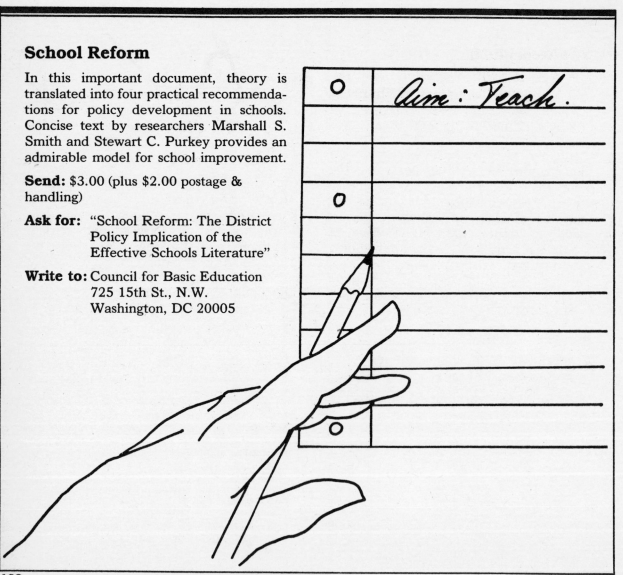

School Reform

In this important document, theory is translated into four practical recommendations for policy development in schools. Concise text by researchers Marshall S. Smith and Stewart C. Purkey provides an admirable model for school improvement.

Send: $3.00 (plus $2.00 postage & handling)

Ask for: "School Reform: The District Policy Implication of the Effective Schools Literature"

Write to: Council for Basic Education
725 15th St., N.W.
Washington, DC 20005

The Stepchild of American Education

Although in-service training ought to be a vitally important part of the preparation of teachers to meet their responsibilities, it has been called the stepchild of American education. The implication is unfortunate, not only because many teachers enter their profession inadequately prepared, or because declining enrollments mean that the schools will depend increasingly on "old" teachers who need "retreading." The fact is that good teachers develop their competence during the course of experience. Peter Greer, superintendent of schools in Portland, Maine, expounds on his views in this important 24-page paper.

Send: $2.00 (plus $2.50 postage & handling)

Ask for: "Education's Stepchild, In-service Training"

Write to: Council for Basic Education
725 15th St., N.W.
Washington, DC 20005

Academic Therapy

Diagnosing and teaching the learning-disabled child are often delicate and difficult even for the most experienced professionals. Academic Therapy Publications provides tests, methods of interpretation, software, special publications, and numerous other teaching aids to help facilitate the complex issues and teaching processes involved in working with learning-disabled children. Their catalog is an invaluable reference not only for specialists, but for teachers of all subjects.

Send: a postcard

Ask for: a catalog

Write to: Academic Therapy
Publications
20 Commercial Blvd.
Novato, CA 94947

Peace and Education

In her world-famous paper on peace and education, Maria Montessori calls for a scientific study of peace. She suggests that if we wish to set about the sane psychical rebuilding of mankind, we must go back to the child. We must, she says, turn to the child as "an inspired being, a regenerator of our race and of society." An inspirational paper for any educator.

Send: 35¢

Ask for: X011 "Peace and Education"

Write to: American Montessori Society
150 Fifth Ave.
New York, NY 10011

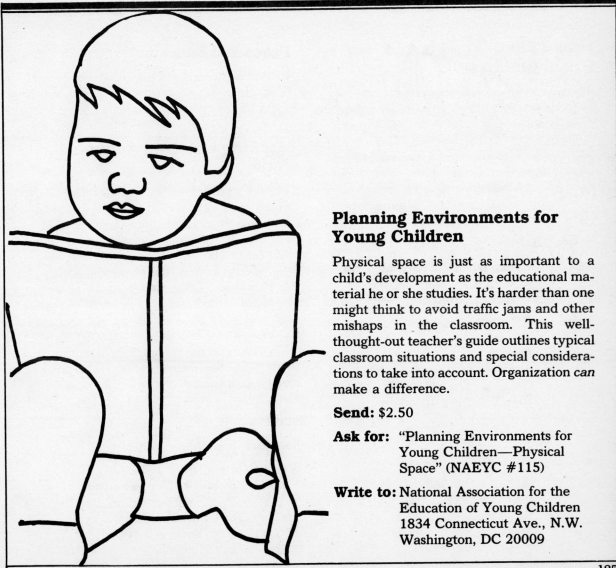

Planning Environments for Young Children

Physical space is just as important to a child's development as the educational material he or she studies. It's harder than one might think to avoid traffic jams and other mishaps in the classroom. This well-thought-out teacher's guide outlines typical classroom situations and special considerations to take into account. Organization *can* make a difference.

Send: $2.50

Ask for: "Planning Environments for Young Children—Physical Space" (NAEYC #115)

Write to: National Association for the Education of Young Children
1834 Connecticut Ave., N.W.
Washington, DC 20009

Urban Environments and Urban Children

The quality of education in city schools has been the subject of much question and research in the past few years. This document by James Garbarino and Margaret C. Plantz is an important aid to understanding the unique problems and educational needs of children growing up in urban environments. Teachers and administrators will find this study enlightening.

Send: $2.00

Ask for: Urban Diversity Series No. 69: "Urban Environments and Urban Children"

Write to: ERIC Clearinghouse on Urban Education
Box 40
Teachers College
Columbia University
New York, NY 10027

Teaching Children About Money

Children's attitudes about money are being formed well before most parents think of preparing them to handle monetary questions. Such influences as television and other kids who have either a lot or very little money have a significant impact, and this pamphlet is designed to make parents aware of these things. It raises such pros and cons as whether or not to give allowances and has helpful answers to 15 questions parents commonly ask about shoplifting, borrowing money, and using money as a means of reward and punishment.

Send: $1.00

Ask for: pamphlet no. 593

Write to: Dept. FTT
Public Affairs Pamphlets
Public Affairs Committee, Inc.
381 Park Ave. South
New York, NY 10016

ou in house

out	pound
loud	shout
noun	scout
found	mountain
sound	fountain

Bilingual Education in the United States

With ever-increasing numbers of non-English-speaking children entering the U.S. school systems, bilingual education has become a serious question. This study provides background material and an interesting perspective, including past and present progress, problems, and possible solutions.

Send: $2.00

Ask for: "Urban Diversity Series No. 68: "Bilingual Education in the United States—A View from 1980"

Write to: ERIC Clearinghouse on Urban Education
Box 40
Teachers College
Columbia University
New York, NY 10027

Susan Osborn is a freelance writer and
part-time teacher